TRIBULATION SALVATION

JESUS STILL SAVES

"...he deceived them that had received the mark of the beast, and them that worshipped his image."

***Tribulation Salvation**—Jesus Still Saves!*
Copyright ©2020
McCowen Mills Publishers
All rights reserved
Printed in the United States of America
Text Design: Rick Quatro (Carmen Publishing Inc., Hilton, NY)
Jacket Design: Mardis Graphic Communication & Design

ISBN 978-1-942452-08-9

ALL RIGHTS RESERVED. No part of this book may be reproduced or transmitted in any form or by any means—graphic, electronic or mechanical, including photocopying, recording, or by any information storage and retrieval system—without permission in writing from the publisher. However, it is the desire of the author to disseminate this information so permission is granted to copy a page for study so long as the copy includes credit.

SCRIPTURE QUOTATIONS FROM the King James Bible need no permission to quote, print, preach, or teach. For clarity, all scripture is in italics with reference and any emphasis in bold print. Any deviation from the King James Bible is not intentional.

McCowen Mills Publishers

Dr. Douglas D. Stauffer, President
1512 East John Sims Pkwy, Suite 346
Niceville, Florida 32578
Website: *www.KJV1611.com*
Email: *Doug@BibleDoug.com*
Phone: (866) 344-1611 (toll free)

Faith Independent Baptist Church

Pastor Doug Stauffer
1309 Valparaiso Blvd., Niceville FL 32578
Website: *www.FaithNiceville.com*
Phone: (850) 678-4387

DOUG STAUFFER, PhD

Author of *One Book Rightly Divided*

TRIBULATION SALVATION

JESUS STILL SAVES

"...he deceived them that had received the mark of the beast, and them that worshipped his image."

Dedication

THIS VOLUME IS affectionately dedicated to my faithful wife, Judy. Thank you for your encouragement and understanding as God tasked me to write yet another book. No man will ever complete the work of God so the sacrifice continues. My prayer is that you will be richly rewarded in this life and eternally rewarded in the life to come. I could never do the work without your faithful support!

"...but as his part is that goeth down to the battle, so shall his part be that tarrieth by the stuff: they shall part alike" **(1 Samuel 30:24b).**

I WOULD ALSO LIKE to expand this dedication to those who truly want to know the truth of scripture. Without lovers of truth, there would be no need to write any Bible-based books. A special thank you toward those who have charged, and encouraged, and strengthened us though your prayers, input, and support. God knows who you are and so do we!

"But the hour cometh, and now is, when the true worshippers shall worship the Father in spirit and in truth: for the Father seeketh such to worship him. God is a Spirit: and they that worship him must worship him in spirit and in truth" **(John 4:23-24).**

Works by the Author

Co-authored books by Douglas D. Stauffer/Andrew B. Ray:

- *One Book Rightly Divided*—Prophetic Edition **(2018, 844 pages, ISBN: 978-1-942452-05-8)**
- *When the End Begins*—Refuting a Rapture in Matthew chapter 24 **(2016, 224 pages, ISBN: 978-1-942452-12-6)**
- *Reviving the Blessed Hope of Thessalonians*—The Rapture Commentary Series Vol. 1 **(2016, 176 pages, ISBN: 978-1-942452-02-7)**
- *Josiah: The Boy Who Would Be King*—A Children's Bible Story and Coloring Book **(2016, 64 pages, ISBN: 978-1-942452-07-2)**
- *Daily Strength 1*—Devotions for Bible Believing Study **(2014, 455 pages, ISBN: 978-1-942452-17-1)**

- *Daily Strength 2*—*Devotions for Bible Believing Study* **(2015, 439 pages, ISBN: 978-1-942452-27-0)**
- *Daily Strength 3*—*Devotions for Bible Believing Study* **(2016, 455 pages, ISBN: 978-1-942452-37-9)**
- *Daily Strength 4*—*Devotions for Bible Believing Study* **(2017, 418 pages, ISBN: 978-1-942452-47-8)**
- *That Blessed Hope*—*Teaching and Defending the Doctrine of the Rapture of the Church* (Co-authored with James Knox and others) **(2017, 286 pages)**

Other books authored by Douglas D. Stauffer:

- *Tribulation Salvation*—*Jesus Still Saves!* **(2020, xx pages, ISBN: 978-1-942452-08-9)**
- *The Illumination of the Book of Revelation*—*Second Edition* **(2019, 245 pages** (OUT OF PRINT)
- *One Book One Authority*—*2,000 Years of Church and Bible History* **(2012, 888 pages, ISBN: 978-0-967701-60-8)**
- *One Book Stands Alone*—*The Key to Believing the Bible* **(2001, 434 pages, ISBN: 978-0-9677016-7-7)**
- *One Book Rightly Divided*—*The Key to Understanding the Bible* **(2006, 276 pages, ISBN: 978-0-967701-61-5)**
- *Freedom's Ring*—*Life, Liberty and the Pursuit of Salvation* **(2008, 400 pages, ISBN: 978-0-967701-69-1)**
- *The DaVinci CON*—*The Great Deception* **(2006, 128 pages)**
- *The Chronicles of Narnia*—*Wholesome Entertainment or Gateway to Paganism?* **(2006, 236 pages)**
- *One Book Stands Alone*—*Roman Catholicism*—*volume 2,* **(2001),** volume 1 (OUT OF PRINT)

Other books, DVDs and CDs on eschatology:

- *Will the Church Go Through the Tribulation?* **(2013, 144 pages)**
- *After the Rapture: Be Not Ignorant Brethren* **(11 CD set, 12+ hours, UPC: 6-89076-67751-6)**
- *Changed by the Book*—*Learn to Study the Bible God's Way* **(7 DVD set, 7+ hours, UPC: 6-89076-44624-2)**
- *In the Last Days* **(4 DVD set, 434 minutes, UPC: 6-89076-677615)**
- *God's Wrath versus the Pre-tribulation Rapture* **(3 DVD set, 384 minutes, UPC: 6-89076-67741-7)**

Acknowledgements

THE AUTHOR WOULD like to express his deepest appreciation to the following: Most preeminently, the precious Lord Jesus Christ for His saving and sustaining grace.

Those who invested the time and effort into my spiritual development, along with the men and women who have been persecuted and sometimes put to death for the faith and their trust in the Saviour and His word. Like many of them, I believe in one authority found in the pages of one book.

My devoted wife for her constant support, encouragement, and understanding through our years of marriage and ministry together. Judy, you are truly God's *second* greatest gift to me **(Romans 6:23)**.

Mr. Rick Quatro his invaluable assistance in formatting the book text. Jeffrey Mardis for his creativity reflected in an impressive cover design. Mrs. Janet Teem for her continued faithfulness in prayer and support.

Lastly, the members of **Faith Independent Baptist Church**, Niceville, Florida for their faithful support and encouragement during this process of writing another book while faithfully serving the Lord with them. When God called me back into the pastorate in January 2019, none would have guessed that he would bring me full circle forty years later to the church that forever impacted me some four decades earlier.

Table of Contents

Dedication . . . . *iv*
Works by the Author . . . . *iv*
Acknowledgements . . . . *vi*
Table of Contents . . . . *vii*
Extended Author Biography . . . . *viii*

Introduction 9
1. A Timely Topic 13
2. Considering Old Testament Salvation 21
3. Knowing the Lord 33
4. Grace & Works Never Mix 41
5. All Saved by the Blood 44
6. Keeping the Commandments 48
7. Who is a Believer? 55
8. Self-Defense Prohibited? 59
9. The Deceived Take the Mark 67
10. How are the Lost Saved? 77
11. Conclusions on Salvation 85
12. False Pauline Preeminence 88

   Postscript 103
   Scripture Index 105
   Word Index 109

Extended Author Biography

DR. DOUGLAS D. STAUFFER is an internationally recognized authority in the fields of Bible history, apologetics, and prophecy. He is a prolific author, having written over twenty books along with numerous writings published in Christian periodicals. Dr. Stauffer was one of two men commissioned in 2003 by **Oxford University Press** to work as contributing and consulting editors on the *New Pilgrim King James Study Bible* which in 2007 became *The Rock of Ages Study Bible*.

Immediately, following high school, Doug served a four-year tour of duty in the United States Air Force stationed at Eglin Air Force Base, Ft. Walton Beach, Florida. He was assigned to the Wing Headquarters at the **33rd Tactical Fighter Wing** and was quickly promoted in rank and position to Assistant Chief of Administration. Upon discharge, he returned home to attend **Penn State University,** graduating with a Bachelor of Science degree in accounting. A few months later he began attending Bible college.

While attending Bible college, Dr. Stauffer passed the CPA exam. He then worked as controller of several organizations. In 1994, he gave up his work as CFO of a multimillion dollar construction company along with managing his own CPA consulting firm when God began dealing with him about dedicating his time more fully to the ministry. Since that time, he has earned his ThM and his PhD in Religion from **International Baptist Seminary.** The Stauffer family traveled hundreds of thousands of miles before being called back into the pastorate in January 2019. In June of that year, he fulfilled his commitments and took over as pastor.

Along with being a frequent guest speaker on radio and television, Dr. Stauffer has served twenty years as an evangelist and fifteen years in the pastorate. He has logged thousands of hours teaching in churches and at the college level. Dr. Stauffer currently serves as pastor of **Faith Independent Baptist Church** of Niceville, Florida. He also serves as a chaplain and National Chief of Staff with the rank of Colonel in the **United States Service Command.** Doug and his wife Judy are blessed with two children, Justin and Heather.

Introduction

MOST ASTUTE BIBLE teachers recognize the several distinctions that exist between salvation before the cross and salvation after it. This phenomenon is known as *Dispensational Salvation*. Briefly, things that are different are not the same. Old Testament salvation, Church Age salvation, and "Tribulation" salvation are not to be equated as uniform and equal because there exist real and definable differences.

For instance, those who take the Mark of the Beast are assured eternal damnation while still alive; no such irreversible condemnation exists during the Church Age. Today, *"where sin abounded, grace did much more abound"* **(Romans 5:20b)**. While obvious and definable distinctions exist, the teacher must avoid emphasizing things beyond the bounds set by God. For instance:

- No one since God first created man can (or will) earn or help to sustain his salvation.
- No one since God first created man can (or will) merit salvation.
- No one since God first created man can (or will) have any type of opportunity to boast for playing even the smallest part of his salvation.
- No one since God first created man has trusted in anything but a merciful and gracious God for his soul's salvation.
- Lastly, heresy in one age has never become respectable doctrine in any other age.

This book primarily focuses upon salvation after the Rapture of the Church. This period, called the time of Jacob's Trouble **(Jeremiah 30:7)**, is like no other ever faced by man. For this reason, God uses extraordinary measures to protect His saints from the soul-destroying deception. Without God's supernatural intervention and exceptional means, God's people could never withstand Satan's deception concerning the Mark of the Beast.

Those who attempt to minimize the extent of the deception and its effectiveness are mere pawns of the Great Deceiver **(2 John 1:7)**. In turn, they will be responsible for the deception and condemnation of future souls. Unfortunately, these same blind guides even attempt to minimize the absolute necessity of God's protective intervention during the most ominous time known to man.

This study delves into pertinent areas of disagreement among Bible teachers in hopes that a better understanding of the entire Bible will aid in grasping how a soul is saved in the future. Some of the many questions answered in this book:

- Why is teaching on salvation after the Rapture so important to get right today?
- What do the two opposing sides teach concerning the salvation of the soul in the future?
- Why is it so important to get the terminology straight concerning the "Tribulation" period versus "Daniel's Seventieth Week"?
- How does studying Old Testament salvation aid in understanding the salvation of a soul following the Rapture?
- Why is such an emphasis placed upon distinguishing between salvation of the soul and physical salvation of the body?
- What terminology does the Bible use to indicate the fruit of salvation in every Age?
- What does the Bible mean when it refers to knowing the Lord?
- Why are grace and works for salvation of the soul considered mutually exclusive from each other?
- What is the identity of the overcomers?
- How do the overcomers overcome?
- Is salvation in the future exclusively by the blood, or does it also include man's good works plus their faith?
- Who keeps the commandments and for what expressed purposes are the commandments kept?
- What are the various titles that God bestows upon "Tribulation" believers?
- How does God supernaturally protect those alive during Daniel's Seventieth Week?
- Why might self-defence be prohibited in the future age?
- How are some teachers propagating a type of Lordship Salvation by adding works to faith for salvation in the future age?
- How are unbelievers induced into taking the Mark of the Beast?
- Why is there such an emphasis concerning deception during Daniel's Seventieth Week?

- Will there be multitudes really saved after the Rapture?
- What does the Bible mean by *"endure unto the end"*?
- What is the *"strong delusion"* sent by God that deceives the lost?
- How are people saved after the Rapture?
- Do those in Daniel's Seventieth Week need to trust in God or trust in self?

This book answers these questions and many many more. Keep in mind that God is not a God of contradictions. Never trust unproven teachings that come from dogmatic assertions based on personal loyalty to anything apart from Almighty God. No individual is worth sacrificing the truth on the altar of misplaced loyalties and manufactured allegiances. God deserves our single-minded devotion.

Keep in mind that preachers are sometimes guilty of making the silliest of faux pas. These gaffes generally happen when men become increasingly insulated from constructive criticism and godly counsel. One such example concerns the contrived distinctions between the so-called laymen (or laity) and clergy (or cleric). No Bible believer should express any acceptance for the false laity/clergy distinctions.

Religious institutions invented these designations to construct the unbiblical hierarchical systems controlled by men at the top. Religions elevated one class of men over another to control the masses by exalting the few. They promoted the so-called clergy over the so-called laity.

Only the novice fails to realize that *"laymen"* and *"laity"* come from God's rebuke concerning the deeds and doctrines of the Nicolaitans which He hates **(Revelation 2:6, Revelation 2:15)**. Any preacher who finds himself on any man-made pedestal or perch should descend with determination and haste. The church is in desperate need of servants and has no more room for self-appointed saviors.

My prayer for this book is twofold: 1) that it will reprove, rebuke, and exhort with all longsuffering and doctrine.

2) Men will let all bitterness, and wrath, and anger, and clamour, and evil speaking, be put away from you, with all malice.

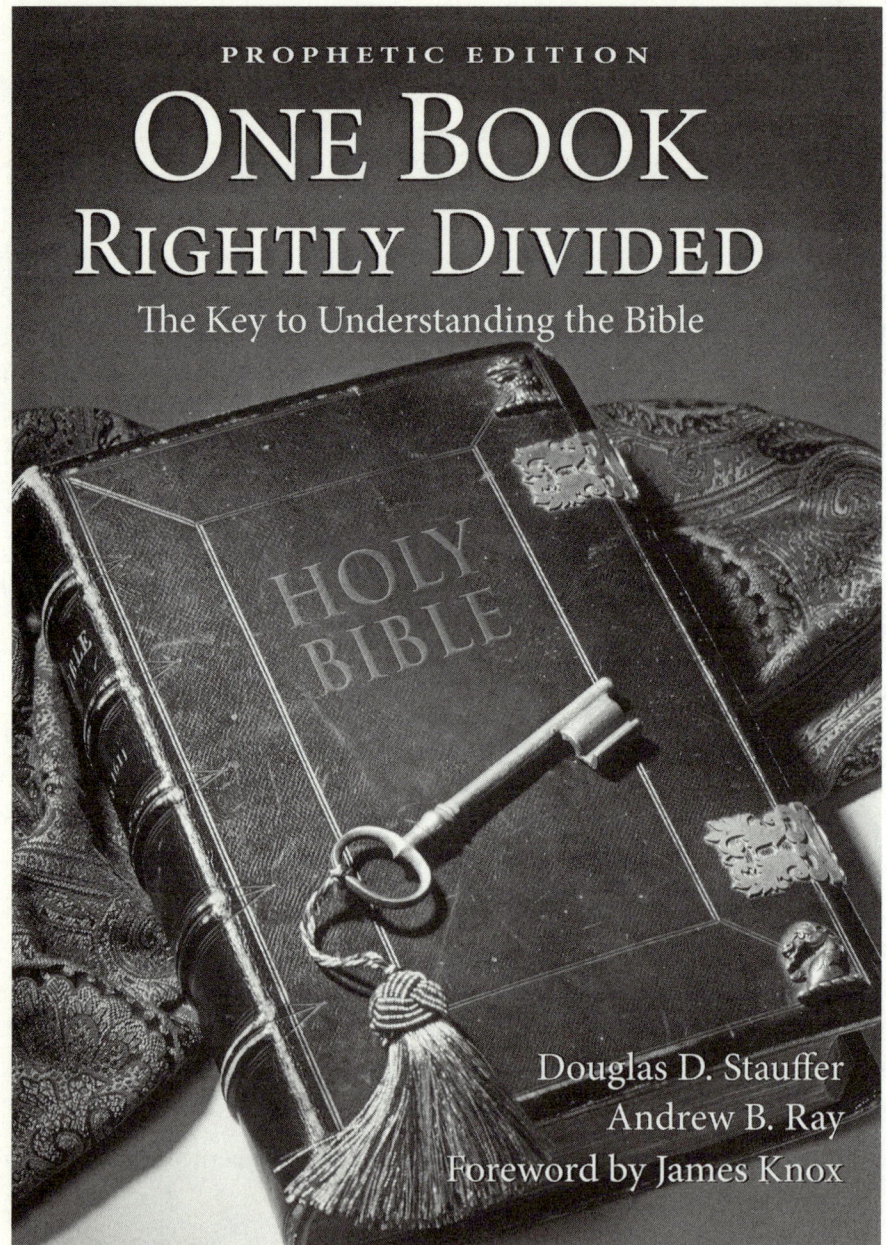

"One Book Rightly Divided: The Prophetic Edition," (844 PAGES), PUBLISHED IN 2018. FOCUSES UPON HOW TO STUDY THE BIBLE DISPENSATIONALLY WITHOUT THE HYPER-DISPENSATIONALISM SO PREVALENT AMONG MANY BIBLE PREACHERS AND TEACHERS IN THIS AGE.

1
A Timely Topic

RECENT DEVELOPMENTS AND societal turmoil have brought a renewed focus concerning prophetic preaching and futuristic events. Christians should positively view this spotlight upon biblical matters since God instructs Christians to be *watching* for Jesus while *waiting* and *working* **(Titus 2:13)**. The events before our eyes, once considered far beyond the spiritual horizon, are developing at lightning speeds.

Christians increasingly believe that these incidents reflect precursors of the events that will take place after the Rapture. Although the timing of the Rapture is one of the most hotly debated subjects in Christendom, it will not be the primary focus of this work. Previous books have extensively addressed that timely issue.[1]

Note: this book does not dabble in newspaper *eisegesis* or any date-setting foolishness that has dishonored the Bible and disgraced the Lord. Although these date-setting prognosticators instruct Christians to watch their calendars, God wants man to focus upon *"that blessed hope."* Man-made charts combined with sensationalistic decrees have caused far too many Christians to stop looking for Christ's appearing EVERY DAY **(Titus 2:13)**. One would think that the lessons of past date-setting blunders would teach the novice not to repeat such foolish endeavors.

Additionally, some men are teaching that people are not to be looking for *"that blessed hope,"* with their eyes instead looking for signs and focused upon Israel. These pontificators are prophesying of an Ezekiel 38-39 war BEFORE the Rapture—so much for imminence. The simplistic answer for the timing of this war is a gap of at least 3½ years after the Rapture and before the commencement of Daniel's Seventieth Week.

---

[1] Read **"Reviving the Blessed Hope"** and **"When the End Begins"** for a discussion of the Pre-, Mid-, and Post-tribulation Rapture teachings and why the authors believe that the Rapture will take place BEFORE any part of the future seven-year period. Both books are available at **www.Bibledoug.com**.

This timing allows for the burning of bodies for seven years *(Ezekiel 39:9)* before the Abomination of Desolation at the midpoint when Israel must flee Jerusalem *(Matthew 14:15-16)*.

No Mere Distraction

The spotlight of this work will be upon salvation after the Rapture. But some exclaim, "Who cares?" Since Christ returns to gather His Church before any part of the commencement of Daniel's Seventieth Week, some Christians consider the topic of salvation following the Church Age a mere distraction. They question the usefulness of expending time and energy discussing "Tribulation"[2] salvation since this subject applies only to those left on earth following the Church's disappearance.

Additionally, no one during the Church Age needs to be concerned about the Mark of the Beast since this Mark cannot and will not be instituted until AFTER the Rapture when the Antichrist appears demanding worship. No one during the Church Age needs to be concerned about the eternal damnation of the soul while still living.

Teachers cannot equate salvation in one age directly with salvation in the next—differences make them incompatible. For instance, the Bible does not indicate that those after the Rapture are adopted or spiritually circumcised. However, the Spirit indwells believers *(1 John 4:4)*, and they are *"in the Lord" (Revelation 14:13)*.

To some Christians, any discussion concerning salvation after the Rapture seems like a moot point. On the surface, that mindset may appear wise and prudent, but unfortunately, it is seriously flawed and heartlessly shortsighted.

---

[2] The **Tribulation period** is an inaccurate designation for the seven-years known as **Daniel's Seventieth Week**. Bible-believers should understand that the Bible never refers to this period as the "Tribulation" or the "Great Tribulation" *(Revelation 7:14)*. For instance, the adjective "great" before the word "tribulation" serves to describe the magnitude of the tribulation experienced during the second half of Daniel's Seventieth Week as compared to the lesser magnitude of tribulation experienced in the first half of the seven years. It is that simple! Man has always suffered tribulation *(Romans 5:3; Romans 8:35; Romans 12:12; 2 Corinthians 1:4; 2 Corinthians 7:4; 1 Thessalonians 3:4; 2 Thessalians 1:4; Revelation 1:9, etc.)*. Bible-believers should be more biblically consistent by referring to this period as Daniel's Seventieth Week and not merely the Tribulation or the Great Tribulation. In these confusing times, prophecy teachers need to strive to be more biblically consistent and stop using these less accurate designations. However, the common term must be used at times because it has become so ingrained in the public's vocabulary.

The topic of so-called Tribulation Salvation has consumed much focus, ink, and energy. Current teachings, whether informative or unwittingly misleading, will inevitably impact those remaining upon earth following the Rapture. Souls in the future will be either positively or negatively influenced depending on whether the preacher's perspective is biblical or anti-scriptural. For this reason, preachers and teachers have a solemn responsibility to ensure that their teachings on this subject, along with others, are biblically sound.

Ensuring the accuracy of teachings that address prophecy following the Rapture is not for the sake of those alive during the present Church Age. Those teachings that endure after the Church's departure will influence those upon the earth. Therefore, teachers today need to get the doctrine right for the sake of those in the future.

Hijacked Truth

Unfortunately, teachers who claim dispensationalism[3] *principally* revolves around soteriology[4] have hijacked this theological system of belief. The saddest fact is that these teachers were taught (and thus incorrectly teach) that Christ's blood sacrifice will NOT be efficacious to save a soul following the Rapture of the Church. ("Efficacious" simply means "effective, efficient or sufficient"). God says that there will be heresies among believers to manifest the true teachers *(1 Corinthians 11:19)*. Yet, how can anyone proclaim such a damnable heresy?

These teachers further limit salvation by grace through faith to the Church Age. They believe that all other periods of history involve faith-plus-works salvation dependent upon a man doing his part to save himself through faith plus his "good" works and efforts.

Dispensational teaching does *not* hang on the hinges of soteriology regardless of what the loudest proponents teach to the contrary. In fact, dispensationalism encompasses ecclesiological aspects (dealing with the church), eschatological aspects (dealing with prophecy) *and* soteriological aspects (dealing with salvation). Legitimate dispensational teaching

---

[3] Dispensationalism is an interpretative system for dividing biblical history into dispensations. These defined periods or ages contain the dispensed truth for those times. These periods contain distinctive administrations, like the Church Age and the "Tribulation." Each of the ages in God's plan has humanity held responsible as stewards during each period. See ***One Book Rightly Divided: The Prophetic Edition*** for a more exhaustive study of dispensationalism.

[4] Soteriology is the study of salvation.

also emphasizes *godly living (Titus 2:12; 2 Peter 2:9)* in this present age, something lacking by far too many of the carnally minded.

Every soul saved depends upon a gracious and merciful God who chooses NOT to reward the sinner according to what he or she eternally deserves. Progressive Revelation[5] simply reinforces this fact. No sinner can stand upon his own merits but must depend upon God extending grace and mercy to all those that believe *(Psalm 130:3-4)*. However, this *does not* mean that the **content of faith** remains the same in each dispensation. For instance, Christ sent the Comforter *after* His final ascension, and God revealed to the apostle Paul the doctrine of Jews and Gentiles placed into one body.

God NEVER equates Christ's shed blood, before or after the cross, on par with anything a man can do. If both (faith and works) are necessary for salvation *at any time*, they are equal. If one (Christ's blood) cannot save without the other (man's works), then God has two incompatible standards for judging man. This philosophy is self-contradictory. A heresy in one dispensation cannot redeem a soul in another dispensation.

If the Rapture were to take place today, many remaining on earth would hear contradictory and confusing teachings on this subject. Yet, God is NOT the author of such confusion *(1 Corinthians 14:33)*. Immediately following the Rapture, there will be people searching for truth through every accessible means—books, internet, etc. The things presently written and taught will likely outlast the Church's departure and affect the souls of those left on the earth. Unfortunately, the erroneous teachings (no matter how sincerely taught) will ultimately become the tools used by Satan to deceive and condemn souls to Hell. There will be many preachers *with blood on their hands,* and this ought not to be so.

Hyper-dispensational Teaching

The most ardent hyper-dispensationalists[6] point to a verse in Romans as the proof text for salvation by works under the Law, and carelessly infer that Christ died in vain.

---

[5] Progressive revelation refers to the gradual, chronological disclosure of divine truth in scripture. Later scriptures and teachings show a clearer view of God's plan and purpose than do earlier scriptures and teachings *(Psalm 119:99)*. The most profound display: The New Testament unfolds the truths that were only obscurely intimated in the Old Testament, eventually allowing the fulness of the entire revelation to be known *(Daniel 12:9)*.

[6] A hyper-dispensationalist is someone who over-divides the Bible and diminishes much of its application to the Church. Primary characteristics of this kind of "teach-

Romans 2:13 *(For not the hearers of the law are just before God, but the doers of the law shall be justified.*

However, God intended this verse to invalidate the false teaching perpetuated by the Jews that merely being a *hearer* of the Law was enough to have fellowship with God. The Law demanded perfect and perpetual obedience (a *doer* of the Law) to avoid the penalty of **physical** condemnation. "Justified" as used in this verse refers to an earthly declaration of doing right, not eternal justification—as in the following passage:

2 Chronicles 6:22 *If a man sin against his neighbour, and an oath be laid upon him to make him swear, and the oath come before thine altar in this house; 23 Then hear thou from heaven, and do, and* **judge thy servants***, by requiting the wicked, by recompensing his way upon his own head; and by* **justifying the righteous***, by giving him according to his righteousness.*

Paul repeatedly affirmed how the *doer* of the Law falls short of justification:

Galatians 2:21 *I do not frustrate the grace of God: for if righteousness come by the law, then* **Christ is dead in vain.**

These same false teachers also spiritualize the following verse:

Romans 3:19 *Now we know that what things soever* **the law saith,** *it saith to them who are under the law: that every mouth may be stopped, and* **all the world may become guilty before God**.

---

er" are eliminating Church Age doctrines from the books of Hebrews, James, and Peter and John's epistles, as well as the four Gospels. This "teacher" *(2 Timothy 4:3; 2 Peter 2:1)* perverts truth and remains unrepentant when shown the error of his teachings. The rationale for not referencing hyper-dispensational works by title or by author:

- It is counterproductive to reward those desperately seeking to bask in the limelight by helping them escape obscurity.

- Directly referencing their teachings offers them a broader platform and higher perceived standing among their disciples.

- The authors of these dubious writings will recognize their addressed errors so maybe they can save face and secretly adjust and align their false teachings with the truth of scripture.

- Their works are not that significant since the author has far more areas of complete agreement with them than disagreement.

- Their names will be irrelevant to those in the future Age seeking truth since the Rapture changes the entire landscape.

God did NOT give the Law of Moses to eternally justify anyone *(Acts 13:39)* because the purpose of God's Law was to condemn the guilty *(1 Timothy 1:9)*.

God sent His precious Son from Heaven's glory because there existed no Law that man could fulfil to become righteous *(Galatians 3:21)*. The "faith-plus-works" teacher confuses New Testament passages concerning eternal matters and salvation *(Romans 4:5)* with the temporal blessings and temporal condemnation of the Old Testament *(2 Chronicles 6:23)*.

It is time to remove the veil and hold these teachers accountable. It is time to warn unsuspecting Bible students lest they become entangled by such blatantly false teachings *(2 Peter 2:1-2)*. More importantly, proclaiming this truth will ensure that these false doctrines do not damn future souls for eternity.

Vindicating the Cults

IF a faith-plus-works-setup is adequate for eternal salvation AT ANY TIME outside the Church Age, then the supposed soteriological WORKS are on par with Christ's blood atonement upon the cross *(Romans 5:11)*. Bible students who deem this position heretical today somehow turn a blind eye toward its acceptance in the future and even the past! According to this reasoning, the blood of Christ without works offers no salvation and no atonement in the future.

Will the false teachers and cultists in the Church Age with their damnable heresies be exonerated if only they miss the Rapture? Think about the seriousness of this false teaching: Church Age heretics only need to live through the Rapture until their works-based false teachings become the acceptable means of salvation.[7] Does God condemn heretical teachings today only to extol their virtues after the Rapture?

---

[7] Imagine a hypothetical scenario at the Great White Throne Judgment: A person shows up at the judgment having trusted in those who taught a faith-plus-works salvation. An inquiry must first be made as to which dispensation he lived to see if he qualified to have his name in the book of life by faith-plus-works *(Revelation 20:15)*, a heresy in the present Church Age. According to this theory, if he lived during the Church Age and missed the Rapture, that which was heresy now will be an acceptable means for the salvation of his soul. Should Christians pray for the Rapture so that the cults and false teachers will be right and hence be saved? Ludicrous, right?

The faith-plus-works teachers would rightfully deem any application of this kind of gospel as heresy during the Church Age. Yet, they align themselves with the cults whom they condemn when they teach faith-plus-works outside the Church Age. They readily and enthusiastically claim works as a component of eternal salvation in other ages and think the scripture supports their position. The Bible *does NOT* support this teaching, and many souls in the future hang in the balance!

It is ill-advised to dismiss this subject as irrelevant unless these "teachers" deem the souls of the future less significant than those of today. Yet, this fact has not diminished people's inclination to offer an assortment of opinions on these future matters. Regardless of one's position on this subject, God offers many explicit and indisputable details concerning the future Age.

Interestingly, the specifics of how someone gets SAVED during Daniel's Seventieth Week (although not equated the same) is one of the main points overlooked by some Bible teachers. Those who hyper-divide Hebrews through Jude into the future "Tribulation" period should consider the next passage.

> **1 Peter 1:18** *Forasmuch as ye know that ye were not **redeemed** with corruptible things, as silver and gold, from your vain conversation received by tradition from your fathers; 19 But **with the precious blood of Christ**, as of a lamb without blemish and without spot:*

Peter plainly states that believers are *"redeemed ... with the precious blood of Christ."* Does the blood become less precious and less efficacious after the Rapture? Does the blood need something to help make it sufficiently salvific?[8] Who was Peter speaking to when he said, *"by whose stripes ye were healed"* **(1 Peter 2:24)**? Does the Rapture diminish the efficacy of the blood? Certainly not. In the future, JESUS STILL SAVES, and salvation is still by the blood. A heresy today remains heretical in the future.

Well, that is the scenario unsuspectingly taught by those who believe works will play a part in the eternal salvation of a soul in the ages to come.

[8] Salvific means *"leading to eternal salvation."*

"*Reviving the Blessed Hope*," (176 PAGES), PUBLISHED IN **2016**. A COMPREHENSIVE STUDY OF FIRST AND SECOND THESSALONIANS WITH IRREFUTABLE PROOF OF THE PRE-TRIBULATION RAPTURE.

2
Considering Old Testament Salvation

I HAVE NEVER HEARD anybody convincingly preach or teach how a man was saved in the Old Testament. Many may pontificate, but few are doing more than clamoring for attention. The most vocal and indeed the most provocative voices belong to those who proclaim faith-plus-works salvation, but the Bible completely disproves this teaching. Faith-plus-works proponents interpret various scriptures that on the surface may appear to indicate a "faith-plus-works-setup" (as they call it), [1] but the teaching is at best inconsistent. This fact remains true even when considering all the so-called problem texts and examining the scripture in their entirety.

Confession Time

Like the faith-plus-works salvation proponents, I too was taught that salvation in every dispensation (outside of the Church Age) included works added to faith. Later I came to understand that certain truths transcend time and contradict contrived manmade dispensational boundaries. The bottom-line: no man has ever, nor will ever have the opportunity to boast for his salvation when standing before a just and holy God for judgment *(Ephesians 2:9)*.

---

[1] This faith-plus-works-setup are the heretical words of one of the proponents of this false teaching. This SETUP is a satanic SETUP and delusion intended to confuse people into thinking they do not need to SOLELY trust in the Lord to be eternally saved in the future. God is merciful, and gracious and only the mercy and grace of God can save a soul—past, present and future. It is a lie to teach otherwise. Works are always the fruit of salvation and never do they initiate the salvation of the soul.

With these truths in mind, it is essential to consider what the scriptures say about salvation for Old Testament saints. Does the Old Testament indicate the *specific means* of salvation? Unlike the New Testament, God did *not* articulate to man an eternal plan of salvation in the Old Testament. Because God offered no clearly defined "plan" back then, many preachers have devised various systems of interpretation. Such is the case with the teaching that Old Testaments saints were *"looking forward to the cross"* when not even the apostles understood the full ramifications of Calvary **(Luke 18:31-34)**.

Regrettably, those proclaiming a faith-plus-works Old Testament salvation can point to the failings of those who believe people were saved by *"looking forward to the cross."* Yet, two wrongs do not make a right. The two extremes on both ends of the spectrum must realign themselves to the middle ground and hold to true biblical doctrine.

Interestingly, groups on both sides of this doctrinal divide have some common ground:

- Nobody entered Heaven save by the blood of Christ
- Nobody entered the eternal presence of God without their sins paid for completely.
- Nobody's sins were taken away by animal sacrifices or living a righteous life.

The fact that most Bible-believers agree on these three points is an important truth that bears further exploration. The reason they both can agree is simple. The scripture indisputably articulates these central truths. However, the same groups often miss the mark when examining other more obscure (and controversial) "doctrines." If people would simply allow the Bible to say what God intended for it to say, rather than privately interpreting it, these kinds of schisms could be eliminated within the body of Christ.

True Bible teaching seeks to eliminate one's private interpretation. God demands all matters to be settled by *"what saith the scripture."* Therefore, it is inconceivable for any preacher to claim that *post-Calvary* saints will be saved by a means that no Old Testament saint could accomplish. The Old Testament is replete with the failures of pre-Calvary "saints." If they could not "live it," why would anyone claim that works plus faith is sufficient for any soul following the cross? Paul refers to those proclaiming such false doctrines as they *"overthrow the faith of some"* **(2 Timothy 2:18)**.

Physical Salvation vs Eternal

Words are the primary tools whereby God communicates His message to man. The Bible uses words to suggest a mental picture or to help the individual reflect upon an experience associated with that word. As a simple example, consider the word "apple" and the image it suggests. There is a mutual understanding of what that word represents. When Spanish speakers say "manzanas," the Spanish speaking individual envisions the same image as an English speaker who understands "apple."

The Bible novice fails to realize the extent of word variations and varying shades of meaning relating to biblical terminology. Yet, this level of understanding is crucial for the Bible-believing Christian who is to *"study to shew* (himself) *approved unto God."* Nevertheless, the inexperienced Bible student frequently elevates his biases by failing to allow words to express God's intended meaning. He often misses much biblical truth because of how *he defines* terms and understands meanings.

The faulty lens through which he views things further compounds these limitations. When the driving motivation is a desire for approbation from peers and mentors, these limitations grow worse. He misses the light of scripture, and his error moves from carelessness to carnality **(1 Corinthians 3:3-4)** and sometimes even heresy.

Like a resolute Calvinist, the misguided hyper-dispensationalist limits specific passages to what he has been taught by his mentors and deemed acceptable by his peers. This same pitfall holds for those espousing that everyone before Calvary was *"looking forward to the cross."* Each group points to the shortcomings of the other. Each fails to realize that both are guilty of elevating their own opinions above the scripture rather than allowing God to speak truth through His word.

With these issues in mind, a short study of the word "salvation" should help to understand the depths and variations of word meanings in scripture. Bible students should strive to determine what the word means and not allow man's interpretations to constrain them. What happens when most Bible students hear the word "salvation?" They immediately think (and rightfully so), "getting to heaven" or "Jesus Christ."

Yet, the shallowness of these thoughts is counterproductive. Delving a little deeper into the word of God helps the student to grasp the proper contextual meanings.

The earliest books of the Bible are a good starting point. These books reference being "saved" or having "salvation." In the following passage from Exodus, the context defines "salvation" as the preservation of life (not eternal security).

> ***Exodus 14:13*** *And Moses said unto the people, Fear ye not, stand still, and see the **salvation** of the LORD, which he will shew to you to day: for the Egyptians whom ye have seen to day, ye shall see them again no more for ever.*

This passage does not refer to the soul's salvation from an eternity in Hell. It refers to the children of Israel's deliverance from their enemies—Pharaoh and his armies—who sought to persecute and destroy them.

> ***Exodus 14:30*** *Thus **the LORD saved Israel** that day out of the hand of the Egyptians; and Israel saw the Egyptians dead upon the sea shore.*

Every astute Bible student would agree that the context is not a reference to God giving anyone eternal life. It referred to God delivering the children of Israel from the grip of a tyrant. In the next chapter, they sang about their deliverance.

> ***Exodus 15:2** The LORD is my strength and song, and he **is become my salvation**: he is my God, and I will prepare him an habitation; my father's God, and I will exalt him.*

This concise study proves why the meanings of words within their context is so crucial. Many well-meaning preachers have proclaimed that Noah was "saved" by building a boat. This statement sounds reasonable until one explores the full implications of such a statement. What does the individual mean when he says this? Does he intend to imply or outright proclaim that Noah obtained some *spiritual benefit* following death through his *faith and works* of building the ark? Hopefully, not! Noah built the ark to save his family *from drowning*. The Bible nowhere equates this "salvation" as deliverance from HELL FIRE! Proclaiming such a thing clouds the truth and elevates one's private interpretation to the throne of one's own making.

Salvation throughout the Old Testament is always *physical deliverance*. Never once (with biases kept in check) will the Bible student find that salvation in the Old Testament refers to eternal life. Yet, when teachers spiritualize Old Testament passages with application to post-Calvary saints, the real context gets clouded:

> **Psalm 13:5** *But I have trusted in thy mercy; my heart shall* **rejoice in thy salvation.**
>
> **Psalm 27:1** *The LORD is my light and* **my salvation***; whom shall I fear? the LORD is the strength of my life; of whom shall I be afraid?*
>
> **Psalm 51:12** *Restore unto me* **the joy of thy salvation***; and uphold me with thy free spirit.*

Many have taught these verses with *spiritual* application to admonish believers to find joy in their salvation. That can be a good thing! Christians should enjoy their salvation, but that is not the doctrinal context of these passages. Teaching that these verses *doctrinally* refer to Christ's sacrifice upon the cross is taking the application beyond its intended context. Additionally, those teaching that these verses *doctrinally* refer to eternal life ignore their real meaning.

Unfortunately, Bible students are often easily tempted to read every biblical reference to "salvation" as being "the gospel of Jesus Christ." Yet, the *faithful* Bible student ALWAYS allows context to determine the meaning. God permits truth to be spiritually applied, but NEVER at the expense of what the verse means *doctrinally* and contextually.

The diligent Bible student recognizes and accounts for God's promise of *physical salvation* to the Jews in the Old Testament. This distinction is important. Did God ever make a promise to them concerning eternal life through the Law? Did He promise them a home in Heaven through the keeping of the commandments? No, on both accounts! The only promises that the Lord gave them included the granting of **physical** health, **physical** life, **physical** deliverance and **physical** blessings. Just read the Bible:

> **Leviticus 26:3** *If ye walk in my statutes, and keep my commandments, and do them;* 4 ***Then I will give you rain*** *in due season, and the land shall yield her increase, and the trees of the field shall yield their fruit.*

> **Deuteronomy 30:9** *And the LORD thy God* **will make thee plenteous** *in every work of thine hand, in the fruit of thy body, and in the fruit of thy cattle, and in the fruit of thy land, for good: for the LORD will again rejoice over thee for good, as he rejoiced over thy fathers: 10* **If thou shalt hearken** *unto the voice of the LORD thy God,* **to keep** *his commandments and his statutes which are written in this book of the law, and if thou turn unto the LORD thy God with all thine heart, and with all thy soul.*

What did God give to people in the Old Testament? God gave the nation of Israel the Law. The plan that He gave them was, *"this do, and thou shalt live."* God prolonged their lives when they did what He prescribed in the Law. Deuteronomy gives the promise of blessing for obedience and the warning of a curse for disobedience.

> **Deuteronomy 30:15** *See, I have set before thee this day* **life and good, and death and evil***; 16 In that I command thee this day to love the LORD thy God, to walk in his ways, and to keep his commandments and his statutes and his judgments,* **that thou mayest live and multiply***: and the LORD thy God shall* **bless thee in the land** *whither thou goest to possess it.*

The promise for faithful obedience is *"life and good,"* yet the passage also pronounces the warning concerning the curse for disobedience. It involves *"death and evil."* Do right and *"live and multiply"* and be blessed in the land. Keep reading:

> **Deuteronomy 30:17** *But if thine heart turn away, so that thou wilt not hear, but shalt be drawn away, and worship other gods, and serve them; 18 I denounce unto you this day,* **that ye shall surely perish***, and that ye shall* **not prolong your days upon the land***, whither thou passest over Jordan to go to possess it.*

What is the context of "living"? Is it a promise of eternal bliss in Heaven or *physical longevity* in the Land? The Bible-believer answers correctly. The context refers to the PHYSICAL and not the eternal! Disobedience means they will PERISH (i.e. die). What does the context infer? *Only physical longevity.*

Remember there are ditches on both sides of the highway. The other group finds themselves in the ditch on the opposite side of the road.

Those who proclaim that everyone before the cross was *"looking forward to the cross"* for salvation cannot find biblical proof for this teaching. Interestingly, the broader context of Deuteronomy chapter 30 offers further insights. What better place than here for God to express His offer of eternal life through the gospel of the grace of God through faith in Jesus Christ? Yet, the Bible does not say that nor infer it.

> ***Deuteronomy 30:11 For this commandment which I command thee this day, it is not hidden from thee****, neither is it far off. 12 It is not in heaven, that thou shouldest say, Who shall go up for us to heaven, and bring it unto us, that we may hear it, and do it? 13 Neither is it beyond the sea, that thou shouldest say, Who shall go over the sea for us, and bring it unto us, that we may hear it, and do it? 14* **But the word is very nigh unto thee, in thy mouth, and in thy heart, that thou mayest do it.**

The apostle Paul quotes this same passage in Romans chapter 10 concerning the gospel! God did not give them the gospel that we know and understand today in Deuteronomy. There is no reason to speculate that God was keeping it a secret from them or that it passed from one generation to the next only orally. God knew that He would use the Old Testament later to propagate the gospel of Jesus Christ, but historically, nobody was *"looking forward to the cross"* because nobody understood it. **God gave Israel the Law to enable them as a nation to live upon the earth (in the Land). God intended the Law to teach them the character of God and never meant for it to save a soul from eternal damnation.**

> ***Exodus 16:4*** *Then said the LORD unto Moses, Behold, I will rain bread from heaven for you; and* **the people shall go out and gather a certain rate every day, that I may prove them, whether they will walk in my law, or no.**

Everyone needs parameters to follow, and God proved Israel with His Law. God did not give these laws to *justify* anyone (eternally), and if He did, then a man could *pay for his salvation*. Look at the next verse and consider that point!

> ***Exodus 21:30*** *If there be laid on him a sum of money,* **then he shall give for the ransom of his life** *whatsoever is laid upon him.*

To what life was the LORD referring? Certainly not eternal life! Consider this truth carefully. If a man breaking the Law and dying was eternally damned, then Exodus chapter 21 made provision for a man to BUY his salvation. Preposterous! The fact is that breaking God's Law could bring an early death but not sure damnation of the soul. False religion teaches that a man can buy his way out of damnation, as illustrated in the false doctrine of "purgatory." Those who pervert the purpose of the Law align themselves with the teachings of the damnable cults and false religions.

Very few people attempted to live out the truth of the Law. The scripture and Israel's history bear out this fact. God's message to them was not a hidden, secret message of the gnostics; it was not in some distant location or outer space; God embedded it within the human conscience given to every man. These men all died because no mere mortal could ever fulfil the God-given Law. Jesus said:

Matthew 5:17 *Think not that **I am come** to destroy the law, or the prophets: I am not come to destroy, but **to fulfil.***

Old Testament saints may have even been able to keep the Law for a time, but until the Lord Jesus Christ, nobody was able to fulfil the Law in its entirety without error.

Proverbs 28:4 *They that forsake the law praise the wicked: but such as **keep the law** contend with them.*

Proverbs 28:7 Whoso keepeth the law *is a wise son: but he that is a companion of riotous men shameth his father.*

Proverbs 29:18 *Where there is no vision, the people perish: but he that **keepeth the law,** happy is he.*

The Lord's conversation with the rich young ruler reinforces this truth. Frequently, the Lord answers a question with a question (verses 17 and 18) because consideration of the answer leads to an understanding of higher truths.

Mark 10:17 *And when he was gone forth into the way, there came one running, and kneeled to him, and asked him, Good Master, **what shall I do that I may inherit eternal life?** 18 And Jesus said unto him, **Why callest thou me good?** there is none good but one, that is, God. 19 Thou knowest the commandments, Do not commit adultery, Do not kill, Do not steal, Do not bear false witness, Defraud not, Honour thy father and mother. 20 And he answered and said unto* *him, Master, all these have I observed from my youth. 21 Then Jesus beholding him loved him, and said unto him, One thing thou lackest: go thy way, sell whatsoever thou hast, and give to the poor, and thou shalt have treasure in heaven: and come, take up the cross, and follow me. 22 And he was sad at that saying, and went away grieved: for he had great possessions. 23 And Jesus looked round about, and saith unto his disciples, How hardly shall they that have riches enter into the kingdom of God!*

The Lord ignores the exact question posed by this rich young ruler because He desires to address a greater truth. *He did not lie to this man—* He did not tell him he could have eternal life by keeping the commandments or selling everything and giving it to the poor. The Lord simply told the rich man to forsake all and follow Him. If he had done what the Lord told him to do, he would have received further exposure to the teachings and truths propagated by the one who was the way, *"the truth and the life" (John 14:6)*! He would have found the answer for which he inquired.

Also, consider the lawyer who asked the Lord Jesus Christ the same type of question in Luke chapter 10.

Luke 10:25 *And, behold, a certain lawyer stood up, and tempted him, saying, Master,* **what shall I do to inherit eternal life***? 26 He said unto him, What is written in the law? how readest thou? 27 And he answering said, Thou shalt love the Lord thy God with all thy heart, and with all thy soul, and with all thy strength, and with all thy mind; and thy neighbour as thyself. 28 And he said unto him, Thou hast answered right:* **this do, and thou shalt live.**

Once again, the Lord Jesus Christ did not tell the lawyer that he could "live forever" but that he would "live." The Old Testament contains this same promise throughout the Law. Those who kept the statutes retained their *physical lives* and extended them. Yet, no matter how long they lived, they all eventually died.

Blameless in the Law

The Bible only mentions three people as being "blameless" concerning the Law, and none of them passed the requirement laid out by God

Almighty. The first two were Zacharias and Elisabeth (the parents of John the Baptist), and the other was the Apostle Paul.

Luke 1:6 *And they were both righteous before God, walking in all the commandments and ordinances of the Lord* **blameless.**

Philippians 3:4 *Though I might also have confidence in the flesh. If any other man thinketh that he hath whereof he might trust in the flesh, I more: 5 Circumcised the eighth day, of the stock of Israel, of the tribe of Benjamin, an Hebrew of the Hebrews; as touching the law, a Pharisee; 6 Concerning zeal, persecuting the church;* **touching the righteousness which is in the law, blameless.**

Like all others, their faith was expressed outwardly through their faithfulness. Why then did God refer to them as *"blameless"*? Their commitment to obey the Lord consistently by faith merited the LORD's bestowal of honour upon them. If their blamelessness could have earned their way to heaven by faith-plus-works, then we should be able to point to them as examples of this fact. However, no such case exists. Their willingness to obey the Law and offer Jewish sacrifices when they failed did not ever *merit them eternal life.*

Old Testament biblical "salvation" is *temporal in nature* and *physical in its deliverance* as reflected by the context. The only provable setting in which salvation is permanent and eternal is when an individual puts his faith in the Son of God, the Lord Jesus Christ (post-Calvary). The Bible does not point to any individual or group who trusted in Christ's shed blood *before the cross.*

In addition to the word "salvation," other words are equally misunderstood and misapplied. The word "justification" has the same misconceptions. Post-Calvary justification is the permanent, eternal declaration of the sinner to be righteous (New Testament). However, the use of "just" and "justification" does not always refer to eternal matters. It can also be applied to temporal matters of judgment and has nothing to do with eternal life.

Deuteronomy 25:1 *If there be a controversy between men, and they come unto judgment, that the judges may judge them; then they shall* **justify the righteous,** *and condemn the wicked.*

> **1 Kings 8:32** *Then hear thou in heaven, and do, and judge thy servants, condemning the wicked, to bring his way upon his head;* **and justifying the righteous**, *to give him according to his righteousness.*

This type of justification would be the same context as James chapter 2 concerning God's declaration of Abraham being a righteous man. He acted upon the faith that he had and obeyed the LORD and was declared to be *just in his actions*. Yet, the permanent, eternal justification which yields eternal life is ONLY FOUND through faith in the shed blood of the Lord Jesus Christ post-Calvary and not before.

> **Romans 3:28** *Therefore we conclude that a man is* ***justified by faith without the deeds of the law.***

A Copout: An "Element" of Faith and Works

Some Bible teachers consider the statements in Ezekiel as contradicting the premise of this booklet. That's unfortunate for them. One such passage is found in **Ezekiel 3:23**, *"When a righteous man commits iniquity, he will die in his sin!"* Yet, Ezekiel is a post-exilic prophet who wrote years after God gave the Law to Moses! For a preacher to use the Ezekiel passage as a *plan of salvation*, he must first prove that God gave this teaching in the original commandments to the nation of Israel.

Where did God command such things in the Law? It occurs nowhere. If this were the plan of salvation in the Old Testament, then surely God would have dispensed it when He gave the Law to Moses. However, every **honest** Bible student knows that no such text exists in any of the books of Moses. Is it reasonable to think that God waited a thousand years after the giving of the Law to show the Jews His plan of eternal salvation for them? Think about that for a moment.

The disingenuous Bible student fails to see the problems associated with using texts from Ezekiel to fabricate proof for his private interpretation. Ezekiel chapters 3, 18, and 33 should be believed as they are written and not wrested out of their context to make them "prove" a false teaching.

Yet, there are Bible teachers who promote this false teaching that Ezekiel provides proof for Old Testament works-plus-faith salvation. This method of Bible interpretation is equivalent to reading the New Testament into the Old Testament. Such is the case when **Romans 2:7** is yanked from the New Testament to offer a bogus plan of salvation for the Old Testament Gentiles which God never articulates a single time throughout the Old Testament.

Preachers could avoid much confusion if they remembered the simplest of Bible truths. For example, the Pentateuch is the giving of the Law while the rest of the Old Testament serves as the narrative of Israel's responsibility to obey it.

Other preachers adjust their phraseology to say there is an "**element of faith and works**" in the Old Testament offering eternal salvation to the doer. Yet, these same preachers refuse to recognize that an **element** of faith and works also exists in the New Testament. God, in every age, has always required faith and that faith produces action.

Faith and works should be the *characteristic* of every follower of God regardless of the dispensation. Every Christian's life is defined by faith in God's word and his obedience to it. Those claiming to be Bible-believers but unwilling to practice biblical principles are not living by faith. Thus, the entire Bible contains an "element" of faith and works.

James 2:18 *Yea, a man may say, Thou hast faith, and I have works: shew me thy faith without thy works, and **I will shew thee my faith by my works.***

God is looking for those who will believe His word and act accordingly. Shamefully, too many "Bible-believers" fail to live right because they *wrongly* divide verses that instruct holy and right living. Such practice cannot be rightly dividing the word as it is the antithesis of sound doctrine and a spiritual life. Those who refuse to live according to the Bible are not Bible-believers.

3
Knowing the Lord

WORDS ARE CERTAINLY important; thus, God uses specific expressions to convey His truths to man. For instance, God's word frequently uses phraseology like *knowing the Lord* in both Testaments to distinguish between saved and lost people.

A Right Relationship

Those identified as KNOWING the LORD have a proper relationship with God; the inverse relationship exists for those who do not KNOW the Lord. The evidence of such a link to the Lord is the individual's desire to follow the Lord. When the Lord Jesus Christ entered the world, John gave testimony to this truth, pointing to a world that KNEW NOT God.

> ***John 1:10** He was in the world, and the world was made by him, **and the world knew him not**. 11 He came unto his own, and his own **received him not**. 12 But as many as received him, to them gave he power to become the sons of God, even to them that believe on his name: 13 Which were born, not of blood, nor of the will of the flesh, nor of the will of man, but of God.*

John testified that God the Son came into a world that KNEW HIM NOT and received Him not. Yet, Christ's purpose was to reconcile those who would believe in Him. Those who received Him were given the power to become the sons of God, thus entering an eternal family relationship with God. The Bible describes this relationship as those who "know Him."

God's word expresses a direct correlation between *receiving* the Lord and *knowing* the Lord. It is essential to recognize and fully comprehend this association and description. The passage from John pinpoints the sons of God: they are those who are born of God (or born again).

The Fruit of Salvation

Now consider the Old Testament canon of scriptures which expresses the same concept concerning knowing God and offers the necessary insights. The Bible describes those who lived wickedly and lived for themselves as people who did not *know the Lord*. Their lack of fruit (knowing the Lord) clearly expressed the relationship they lacked.

The sons of Eli serve as a prime example. These two men were priests in the Jewish system of worship, yet their religious position did *not* guarantee them any security concerning salvation. The Bible clearly shows how they filled the spiritual position but failed to know the Lord.

*1 Samuel 2:12 Now the sons of Eli were **sons of Belial; they knew not the LORD**.*

The book of Samuel says the sons of Eli were *"sons of Belial,"* that is, children of the devil. The critical point to notice is that the Bible directly correlates this designation with those who did not KNOW the Lord. Recognizing this connection becomes a means of understanding the truth of Old Testament salvation. **However, KNOWING God in this context does NOT merely refer to an act of intellectual knowledge.**

The sons of Eli serve as a negative example, while another central figure during the same period sheds further light upon this truth. The Bible says that the young man Samuel did not YET know the LORD.

*1 Samuel 3:7 Now **Samuel did not yet know the LORD**, neither was the word of the LORD yet revealed unto him.*

This statement implies that Samuel would later come to KNOW the LORD. It seems impossible for Samuel not to have known *about* the LORD, considering he lived in the Temple. Knowing the Lord in this context is all about relationship—not intellectual comprehension. The sons of Eli knew *of* the LORD but did not have a *relationship* with Him. Samuel would come to know the LORD in a personal sense later in life.

The sons of Eli were said to be children of Belial. How does the Bible define the *"children of Belial"*? Simply put, they were unbelievers who rejected God.

*Deuteronomy 13:13 Certain men, **the children of Belial**, are gone out from among you, and have withdrawn the inhabitants of their* city, saying, **Let us go and serve other gods**, which ye have not known;

These *"children of Belial"* chose not to know the LORD and chose to serve other gods. The Bible uses another term for unbelievers—that of "heathen." Again, the Bible directly associates the heathen with those who did not KNOW the LORD.

*Jeremiah 10:25 Pour out thy fury upon **the heathen that know thee not**, and upon the families that call not on thy name: for they have eaten up Jacob, and devoured him, and consumed him, and have made his habitation desolate.*

*Jeremiah 9:3 And they bend their tongues like their bow for lies: but they are not valiant for the truth upon the earth; for they proceed from evil to evil, and **they know not me**, saith the LORD.*

God offers a consistent pattern throughout the Bible. For instance, when the Pharaoh of Egypt proclaimed to KNOW NOT the LORD, he was simply declaring his standing as an unbeliever. Of course, this showed that he had an intellectual knowledge of God but no relationship with Him.

*Exodus 5:2 And Pharaoh said, Who is the LORD, that I should obey his voice to let Israel go? **I know not the LORD**, neither will I let Israel go.*

Joshua led the people of Israel after Moses died. Unfortunately, after Joshua's death, much of the nation forsook the Lord and followed other gods. The Bible describes the generation as one that *"knew not the LORD."* Of course, they knew that He existed, but they did not know Him in a salvific sense.

*Judges 2:10 And also all that generation were gathered unto their fathers: and **there arose another generation after them, which knew not the LORD**, nor yet the works which he had done for Israel. 11 And the children of Israel did evil in the sight of the LORD, and **served Baalim**: 12 And **they forsook the LORD** God of their fathers, which brought them out of the land of Egypt, and **followed other gods**, of the gods of the people that were round about them, and bowed themselves unto them, and provoked the LORD to anger.*

David specifically gave commandment to his son Solomon to KNOW God. The only means whereby Solomon could know Him was through the right relationship.

*1 Chronicles 28:9 And thou, Solomon my son, **know thou the God of thy father**, and serve him with a perfect heart and with a willing mind: for the LORD searcheth all hearts, and understandeth all the imaginations of the thoughts: if thou seek him, he will be found of thee; but if thou forsake him, he will cast thee off for ever.*

The Bible clearly expresses what it means to KNOW THE LORD: all those who have a relationship with God do so by putting their trust in Him, and that trust continues to blossom.

*Psalm 9:10 And they **that know thy name will put their trust in thee**: for thou, LORD, hast not forsaken them that seek thee.*

How did people in the Old Testament come to know the Lord? The book of Hebrews answers definitively—the only testimony of scripture is **by faith**.

The Hall of Faith

*Hebrews 11:4 **By faith** Abel offered unto God a more excellent sacrifice than Cain, by which he obtained witness that he was righteous, God testifying of his gifts: and by it he being dead yet speaketh.*

*Hebrews 11:5 **By faith** Enoch was translated that he should not see death; and was not found, because God had translated him: for before his translation he had this testimony, that he pleased God.*

*Hebrews 11:7 **By faith** Noah, being warned of God of things not seen as yet, moved with fear, prepared an ark to the saving of his house; by the which he condemned the world, and became heir of the righteousness which is by faith.*

*Hebrews 11:8 **By faith** Abraham, when he was called to go out into a place which he should after receive for an inheritance, obeyed; and he went out, not knowing whither he went.*

The scripture is clear: faith is the prevailing characteristic of Old Testament saints which the unbelievers lacked. The actions of the saints are mentioned, but those actions always resulted from trusting God. Had not God revealed Himself, none of their actions would have been by faith or likely would not have acted at all.

> **Hebrews 11:6** *But **without faith** it is **impossible** to please him: for he that cometh to God must believe that he is, and that he is a rewarder of them that diligently seek him.*

Consider the true story of the rich man and Lazarus in Luke chapter 16. This narrative is pre-Calvary, which means that Lazarus is an Old Testament saint. When Lazarus died, he went to Paradise in the heart of the earth. However, the rich man's soul departed and ended up in Hell.

> **Luke 16:19** *There was **a certain rich man**, which was clothed in purple and fine linen, and fared sumptuously every day: 20 And there was a certain beggar named **Lazarus**, which was laid at his gate, full of sores, 21 And desiring to be fed with the crumbs which fell from the rich man's table: moreover the dogs came and licked his sores. 22 And it came to pass, that the beggar died, and was carried by the angels into Abraham's bosom: the rich man also died, and was buried; 23 And in hell he lift up his eyes, being in torments, and seeth Abraham afar off, and Lazarus in his bosom.*

There is *no mention* of Lazarus' *works* contributing to his landing in Paradise. Yet, we do know that he did *not* end up in the same place as the rich man. What likely separated the two of them following their deaths? Likely, Lazarus pleased God, and the rich man did not. How? The Bible repeatedly and emphatically pointed to faith as the only way to please God. So, it would be wise to conclude that Lazarus too was a man of faith although not mentioned by name in Hebrews chapter 11!

Faith in God and His word is the only means whereby a proper relationship with the Lord can exist. Likewise, relationships are built upon communication, whether between men or between man and God. When one ceases to care about what the other has to say, the relationship ends. Fellowship is severed when there is no more consideration of the viewpoint of the other. God says as much concerning His people.

> **Isaiah 59:2** *But your iniquities have **separated between you and your God**, and your sins have hid his face from you, that he will not hear.*

Restoration with the Creator takes place when men depart from sin by placing their faith in God's word. Works are the result of faith demonstrated and the response to God's salvation. It is essential to understand that works are NEVER the root of salvation but always the fruit of being saved.

Fortunately, knowing and trusting in God has never been limited to those in Old Testament times. This knowing and trusting match the Christian's trust in the Lord after he or she hears the truth of the gospel of the grace of God. Unfortunately, those who hyper-divide the Bible ignore truths God intended for trans-dispensational application.

How to KNOW God

Yet, another truth must garner our attention. The world does not come to know God through worldly wisdom or intellectual means. Neither do they come to know God through any form of personal righteousness. The New Testament is clear—no one can be eternally saved without receiving the Lord Jesus Christ. The Bible says that the light shined to give *"the knowledge of the glory of God"* out of the darkness of this world.

> **2 Corinthians 4:6** *For God, who commanded the light to shine out of darkness, hath shined in our hearts,* **to give the light of the knowledge of the glory of God** *in the face of Jesus Christ.*

Every individual who died lost never knew God. Those still alive but remaining in a lost state *"knew not God,"* until he or she came to see the light at salvation. After salvation, Galatians says that the believers both know God and *"are known of God."* The reason the Bible does not name the rich man in Luke chapter 16 was that God did not know him.

> **Galatians 4:8** *Howbeit then,* **when ye knew not God***, ye did service unto them which by nature are no gods.* 9 **But now, after that ye have known God***, or rather are* **known of God***, how turn ye again to the weak and beggarly elements, whereunto ye desire again to be in bondage?*

Education gives understanding, and it gives intellect but no personal knowledge of the LORD. Unbelievers must *first* hear *about* Him and then receive Him by accepting the validity of that knowledge. Only then will they enter into a *personal* and *intimate* relationship with Him. Thus, God will know them, and they will know Him.

1 Corinthians 1:20 *Where is the wise? where is the scribe? where is the disputer of this world? hath not God made foolish the wisdom of this world? 21 For after that in the wisdom of God* **the world by wisdom knew not God**, *it pleased God by the foolishness of preaching to* **save them that believe**.

The contrast is evident: the lost world does not KNOW God, but believers are enabled to KNOW Him through salvation. God wants all men to be saved and *"to come unto the knowledge of the truth."* Once they come to that knowledge of the truth and believe it, then they will have the ability to KNOW the LORD.

1 Timothy 2:4 *Who will have all men to be* **saved, and to come unto the knowledge of the truth.**

God never exalts a man's intellect. The "knowledge of God" is not knowledge for the sake of learning. It is an understanding of man's relationship to the gospel and receiving that truth that leads to the saving of the soul.

An Ongoing Process

Believing on the Lord Jesus Christ (being born again) is an event (one time), that an individual must experience to go to Heaven. Knowing the Lord begins at salvation and becomes an ongoing process as the believer grows. He knows the Lord at salvation but must mature in his knowledge.

Ephesians 4:15 *But speaking the truth in love, may* **grow up into him in all things**, *which is the head, even Christ:*

The Christian walk is a continuation of maturing in Christ. Peter wrote concerning this very matter.

2 Peter 3:18 *But* **grow** *in grace, and* **in the knowledge of our Lord and Saviour Jesus Christ**. *To him be glory both now and for ever. Amen.*

"*When the End Begins,*" (224 PAGES), PUBLISHED IN 2017. A COMPREHENSIVE STUDY OF MATTHEW CHAPTERS 24 AND 25 (THE OLIVET DISCOURSE) WITH IRREFUTABLE PROOF OF THE PRE-TRIBULATION RAPTURE.

4
Grace & Works Never Mix

PAUL'S TEACHING IS clear. He taught if works could save a man, the individual is NOT saved by grace (and vice versa). There is never any scriptural blending of works plus grace for eternal salvation except in the minds of some men—certainly not in the mind of God.

Mutual Exclusivity

These two elements (works and grace) are opposed to each other concerning salvation. Every spiritual equation teaches that salvific grace plus works of the Law cancel each other out.

> **Romans 11:6** And if by **grace**, then is it **no more of works: otherwise grace is no more grace**. But if it be of works, then is it no more grace: otherwise work is no more work.

By definition, salvation by grace means NO WORKS are involved. Any manmade WORKS salvation setup (whether works alone or by adding works to faith) completely negates God's GRACE. Read the verse again—that is exactly what it says, and that is exactly what it means. All sinners (both in the Old and New Testaments) need God's grace. The book of Romans teaches that any *works* salvation system negates salvation by the grace of a holy, merciful AND GRACIOUS GOD *(Exodus 34:6; 2 Chronicles 30:9; Ezra 9:8-9; Nehemiah 9:17, Psalm 86:15, 103:8, 111:4, 112:4, 116:4-6, 145:8; Joel 2:13; Jonah 4:2, etc.)*.

Imagine anyone teaching that a man could earn His salvation through some form of good works added to his faith. God indwells Christians in the Church Age *(2 Timothy 1:14)*. Unfortunately, most believers prove themselves incapable of consistently keeping the most reasonable New Testament standards, like presenting their bodies as living sacrifices *(Romans 12:1-3)*. It is nonsensical to think that Old Testament saints **with no permanent indwelling Saviour** could fulfil the Law even with its harsher *physical* repercussions. Yet, some well-meaning brethren teach this.

Contradicting the Bible

The hyper-dispensationalist would do well to consider his "Tribulation books"[1] and Paul's admonition to believers. When believers are in need, God tells them to come boldly to Him for help. The Bible NEVER (from Genesis to Revelation) advises anyone to depend upon their own might and strength. Reading the scripture clears up so many false teachings. God's throne of GRACE remains man's supreme remedy during Daniel's Seventieth Week!

*Hebrews 4:16 Let us therefore **come boldly unto the throne of grace**, that we may **obtain mercy, and find grace to help in time of need**.*

*Hebrews 13:6 So that we may boldly say, **The Lord is my helper, and I will not fear what man shall do unto me**.*

Man's greatest hope, now and in the future, necessitates his seeking out mercy and grace from the LORD. God instructs those reading the book of Hebrews to:

---

[1] The adamantly unrepentant hyper-dispensationalist consigns Hebrews through Revelation books as being most applicable to the "Tribulation." When confronted with the fact that these books contain many eternal security passages *(Hebrews 13:5; 1 John 5:13)*, they extract those "Problem texts" from their contexts and apply them to the Church Age only. These teachers claim Church Age doctrines are to be "rightly divided" from the "Tribulation books" but dismissed by those living during the "Tribulation." In other words, they claim eternal security passages apply to the Church Age *within these books* and not to someone during Daniel's Seventieth Week. Another token to their sheer hypocrisy and inconsistency!

Preachers today could deem these inconsistencies as humorous if they were not so potentially damning to future souls. After the Rapture, the world will be suddenly void of Christians. Imagine people on earth fleeing for their lives. According to the hyper-divider, their survival will depend upon going to the Bible and "rightly dividing" it. Does their only hope rest in picking and choosing the right verses within the "right" Bible books? God is not the one that created this confusion—it is manmade and satanically inspired.

- Boldly come to the throne of grace in prayer
- Obtain mercy from a merciful God in time of need
- Find grace from a gracious God in time of need
- Boldly proclaim that the Lord is their helper
- Not fear what man does to them

Because the most vocal preachers have perverted these truths, this teaching may sound foreign to many readers. It is time to be scriptural both in word and deed! The message given to those addressed in the book of Hebrews is: Jesus SAVES! It is Jesus PLUS nothing!

> ***Hebrews 7:22** By so much was **Jesus** made a surety of a better testament. ... 25 **Wherefore he is able also to save them to the uttermost that come unto God by him**, seeing he ever liveth to make intercession for them. 26 For such an high priest became us, who is holy, harmless, undefiled, separate from sinners, and made higher than the heavens; 27 Who needeth not daily, as those high priests, to offer up sacrifice, first for his own sins, and then for the people's: for this he did once, **when he offered up himself.***

> ***Jude 1:24 Now unto him that is able to keep you from falling**, and to present you faultless before the presence of his glory with exceeding joy, 25 **To the only wise God our Saviour**, be glory and majesty, dominion and power, both now and ever. Amen.*

Those so-called "Tribulation" books contradict the very teachings the hyper-dispensationalist proclaims. The two verses above are only a small sampling of the truths hyper-divided by the hyper-dividers. True Bible-believers do not excuse away any Bible verse that proves their teaching false. They adjust their teachings to align them with the Bible. It is time for Bible-believers to believe the Bible no matter how much they are ridiculed or scorned by those they seek to please.

5
All Saved by the Blood

REVELATION CHAPTER 12 tells us that "Tribulation" overcomers (the "brethren" mentioned in verse 10) are those who have trusted in the shed blood of Christ, giving them the testimony of faith.[1] These BRETHREN are **believers,** as opposed to **unbelievers,** who do not overcome. Thus, *"brethren"* refers to those who have trusted in the Lord Jesus Christ. It does not merely apply to Israel or the lost.

> *Revelation 12:11 And they* **[the brethren]** *overcame him by the blood of the Lamb, and by* **the word of their testimony***; and they loved not their lives unto the death.*

Contrary to the faith-plus-works proponents,[2] no one during Daniel's Seventieth Week will be saved based upon their power and ability to withstand Satan's evil onslaught. During the most dreadful time since man's creation, Christ's sacrifice upon the cross will remain sufficient to save every lost soul who trusts in that one blessed payment.

---

[1] The Apostle Paul commended believers when he wrote of the confirmation of *"the* ***testimony*** *of Christ"* to those who were waiting for the *"coming of our Lord Jesus Christ"* **(1 Corinthians 1:6-7)**. See also *"the testimony of God"* **(1 Corinthians 2:1-2)**. Christ told Paul that the Jews would reject his *"testimony"* concerning Christ **(Acts 22:18)**. The *"word of their testimony"* in Revelation corresponds to what a man testifies **(Acts 18:5; 20:21, 24; 23:11; <u>Revelation 6:9</u>; etc.)**

[2] There is one vocally active fringe group that pushes the belief or rejection of faith-plus-works salvation as one of the PRIMARY tests for fellowship. The author has run into many direct confrontations with this small splinter group. In fact, I was taught this faith-plus-works system and regurgitated it in my earliest years. Believing what the Bible says (in its context) enabled the fog to clear and the light of truth to prevail. The change did not happen overnight but methodically transitioned as more truth came to light. Unfortunately, far too many preachers refuse to consider that they may be wrong because they fear man more than they fear God! *"The fear of man bringeth a snare: but whoso putteth his trust in the LORD shall be safe"* **(Proverbs 29:25)**. Others look for any way possible to disregard the Holy Ghost's pricking of their hearts. As they quench the Spirit, darkness prevails.

After the Church's departure at the Rapture, salvation will *not* somehow mutate into man's futile attempts at good work(s) like *trying not to take the Mark*. Unmerited salvation through the Lord Jesus Christ will continue to be God's standard. God's grace, as evidenced by His provision of supernatural protection from deception (discussed later) keeps a soul eternally safe in the future. The Bible is clear: salvation is by the blood, and the brethren overcome *"by the blood of the Lamb."*

The "Works" of their Testimony?

Revelation 12:11 also says *"by the **word** of their testimony."* Bible students should not allow their preconceived doctrinal suppositions to distort their understanding. Forcing this mindset upon the text makes it say the saints overcome by the **WORKS** *"of their testimony."* That is not what the Bible says nor what it implies.

Allowing the Bible to self-define words is the only remedy to interpretive deception. The book of Revelation sheds light on the meaning of *"testimony"* as it occurs eight times in seven verses in Revelation:

- *"the **testimony** of Jesus Christ" **(Revelation 1:2)***
- *"the **testimony** of Jesus Christ" **(Revelation 1:9)***
- Believers *"slain … for word of God, and for the **testimony** which they held" **(Revelation 6:9)***
- The two witnesses *"shall have finished their **testimony**" **(Revelation 11:7)***
- The brethren *"overcame him by the blood of the Lamb, and by the word of their **testimony**" **(Revelation 12:11)***
- The remnant *"which keep the commandments of God, and have the **testimony** of Jesus Christ" **(Revelation 12:17)***
- *"the temple of the tabernacle of the **testimony** in heaven" **(Revelation 15:5)***
- *"thy **brethren** that have the **testimony** of Jesus: worship God: for the **testimony** of Jesus is the spirit of prophecy" **(Revelation 19:10)***

Not one of these eight instances emphasize a man's WORKS. Fortunately, the earliest of English dictionaries (Webster's 1828) offers a clear definition of testimony—*"A solemn declaration or affirmation made for the purpose of establishing or proving some fact."* Believers will be executed after the Rapture (like some are today) because of their TESTIMONY—that being, *"the testimony of Jesus Christ."* Their testimony identified them with the Saviour.

Some Christians struggle with grasping this truth because God's focus after the Rapture again reverts to the nation of Israel, which historically has rejected the Lord Jesus Christ. Yet, the Bible distinguishes between the true brethren and Jewish unbelievers when it says, *"they are not all Israel, which are of Israel"* **(Romans 9:6).**

BELIEVERS, whether Jews or non-Jews, will NOT be Christ-rejecters. The one fact post-Calvary that will remain true even during Daniel's Seventieth Week: *JESUS SAVES!* Teaching salvation changes into some type of faith-plus-works setup is a satanic delusion at its core. Yet, the false teachings of today will dupe many people into trusting this soul-condemning heresy in the future. Who then will be responsible for those deceived souls? The false teachers of today! Read the verse carefully.

Revelation 12:11 And they overcame him *by **the blood of the Lamb**, and by **the word of their testimony**; and they loved not their lives unto the death.*

Notice how this passage points to only TWO aspects for overcoming. Unfortunately, some works plus faith proponents CHANGE this verse in Revelation from *two* to *three* elements for overcoming by reading their pre-conceived notions into the scripture. Remember that every single word of God is essential, even a seemingly insignificant two-letter word like "by."

Overcome BY These Two

The little word "by" indicates that only *two* aspects exist for overcoming—NOT THREE. Reread the verse: the verse says *"BY the blood," "BY the word,"* but it does NOT say BY not loving their lives unto the death. The unscrupulous promoters of a false gospel teach that believers overcome BY not loving their lives unto the death. They wrest the scripture to force them to "prove" their false teachings. They intentionally insert their bias into the verse. They are no more innocent than the Calvinist or the cultist who make the same gross errors in Bible hermeneutics.

The Bible states that those not loving their lives unto THE death do so because they ARE overcomers, not to become overcomers. Again, read the scripture: the believers overcame **BY** two aspects.

1. The believers overcame **BY** the blood of the Lamb.

2. The believers overcame **BY** the word of their testimony.

What is the result of the believers overcoming **BY** these TWO aspects? They loved not their lives unto the death. Not loving their lives unto THE death is the *fruit* of being an overcomer, not the *root* of overcoming.

Why did these believers during Daniel's Seventieth Week *not* love their lives unto THE death? Because they trusted in Christ's blood atonement and God assured them of their salvation **(Hebrews 6:11; Hebrews 10:22)**. Their relationship to God supernaturally protected them from the deception that would otherwise condemn. The reason why knowledgeable Bible teachers teach false doctrine is quite simple. It does not matter how much someone studies the Bible when they FORCE the Bible to prove a false doctrine right.

The WORD of their testimony refers to believers in the future. These believers will have trusted in the blood of the Lamb and have the *"testimony of Jesus,"* and that is sufficient to get them killed. Yet, their testimony affords them access to the supernatural protection of God Almighty. Only those who call upon the name of the Lord will be saved and delivered *(Acts 2:21)*.

6
Keeping the Commandments

SOME OF THE most counterproductive Bible studies occur when people approach God's word with pre-conceived notions. Disaster ensues when their beliefs are both erroneous and rigid. Once the truth is laid aside for flawed interpretations, the Christian becomes entrenched in the ditch of false theology. Once man rejects the truth, the darkness dims the light until there remains no light.

The Spirit of truth is quenched by the egotism of thinking one is never wrong *(John 16:13)*. An excellent example concerns teachers' definitions regarding those who *"keep the commandments of God."* Some hyper-dispensationalists view this phrase as a need to keep God's commandments during Daniel's Seventieth Week to earn one's salvation. The scripture teaches no such fairytale! Only those who elevate pride over truth would continue to hold to such a careless position.

> ***Revelation 12:17*** *And the dragon was wroth with the woman, and went to make war with the remnant of her seed, which* **keep the commandments of God**, *and have the testimony of Jesus Christ.*

Nowhere (Old Testament or New) does the Bible say (or imply) that keeping the commandments is a means of eternal salvation. Nowhere! The Bible plainly and repeatedly teaches the opposite—those who teach otherwise make God a liar. Those claiming to be Bible-believers should strive for consistency rather than plodding along blindly. They try so hard not to end up in one ditch that they veer over into the opposite side and ditch. Preconceived agendas ignore the context and wrest the scripture to teach something the Bible does not teach (i.e. the faith-plus-works-setup). This concept is referred to as *"reading your theology into the text."*

The New Testament phrase *"keep the commandments of God"* with several variations occurs thirteen times—half of which appear in the book of First John.[1] Diligent Bible students consider the context of EVERY usage of a word or phrase before arriving at a conclusion, thus avoiding the temptation to interpret privately.

The Bible offers several unambiguous reasons for keeping God's commandments, and NONE of them involves getting saved or remaining saved—not one. Those who keep the commandments of God exhibit the testimony that they are part of the brethren (called fellowservants and saints). The Bible gives several reasons for keeping God's commandments.

Keep the Commandments of God: For Assurance of Salvation

How does a person know that he knows Jesus Christ? Throughout scripture, God has repeatedly stated that keeping His commandments is a means to gain assurance of salvation. Assurance does *not* come by living like a rebel. Rather, a person receives assurance only by obedience to the word.[2]

> **1 John 2:3** And **hereby we do know that we know him, if we keep his commandments.** 4 He that saith, I know him, and keepeth not his commandments, is a liar, and the truth is not in him.

---

[1] First John is found in that section of scripture of Hebrews through Revelation that is relegated by the hyper-dispensationalist as "Tribulation" books.

[2] Again, the Bible never refers to "keeping the commandments" to bring about a soul's salvation. Only Christ's sacrifice could do such—without any admixture of works. Christians today are to keep the commandments of God and yet fail God daily. However, their identity as believers remain unchanged. The Calvinist says you must persevere, or you were never saved. The true Bible-believer knows that we are simply saved sinners that struggle with the world, the flesh, and the Devil daily. God chastens His children because they are His children **(Hebrews 12:5-8)**. The reason children of God need chastening is because Christians have a tendency to stray from doing what they know to be right. Without God's correcting hand, believers would never be able to live a consistent life.

According to this passage, keeping God's commandments SAVES no one; however, living right and doing right offers clear assurance to the believer that He knows God. This passage provides insights as to why disobedient Christians often struggle with genuine assurance of salvation. Most of those who doubt their salvation miss the assurance stemming from doing right and living right—i.e. doing what God has said to do in His word.

Verse one of First John chapter 5 defines how a person is born of God: NOT by keeping the commandments, but by believing that Jesus is the Christ. The verse goes on to state that all those who love God also love their fellow believers.

> *1 John 5:1 Whosoever believeth that Jesus is the Christ is born of God: and every one that loveth him that begat loveth him also that is begotten of him. 2 **By this we know that we love the children of God, when we love God, and keep his commandments**. 3 **For this is the love of God**, that we keep his commandments: and his commandments are not grievous. 4 For whatsoever is born of God overcometh the world: and this is the victory that overcometh the world, even our faith. 5 Who is he that overcometh the world, but he that believeth that Jesus is the Son of God?*

Verse two states that believers can KNOW they love other believers when they choose to love God and keep His commandments. Those who do *NOT* love their fellow brethren have a testimony from God that they do *NOT* love God. Loving others is much more than a mere expression of words. Verse three defines the love of God as keeping His commandments.

The disobedient may claim to love God, but they do NOT love God when they fail to love others. Verse three concludes by stating that God's commandments are NOT grievous, but they certainly would be if "commandments" in this context referred to the 613 Old Testament laws. They do not refer to keeping the Jewish Law. The apostles knew that their ancestors struggled with keeping God's Law.

> *Acts 15:10 Now therefore why tempt ye God, to put a yoke upon the neck of the disciples, which **neither our fathers nor we were able to bear**?*

Keeping the commandments would undoubtedly be considered grievous if failing to fulfil them brought about a loss of salvation! Keeping the commandments attests to the believer's relationship with God; not how that relationship is achieved or preserved. Only a Bible-rejector would ignore this plain teaching from the scripture to continue to bolster his false doctrine.

Simply put, salvation is all about the Lord Jesus Christ and His shed blood on the cross! That same *"precious blood"* redeems the sinner before the Rapture *and after* the Rapture!

*1 Peter 1:18 Forasmuch as ye know that ye were not **redeemed** with corruptible things, as silver and gold, from your vain conversation received by tradition from your fathers; 19 But **with the precious blood of Christ**, as of a lamb without blemish and without spot:*

The saints during Daniel's Seventieth Week (also called "brethren" and "elect") are the ones who have trusted Jesus Christ. At no point will their salvation be dependent upon themselves (more proof to follow). The brethren in Daniel's Seventieth Week are the believers in Jesus Christ; their salvation is dependent upon the *"faith of Jesus" **(Revelation 14:12)**.*

Keep the Commandments of God: To Get Prayers Answered

The second reason for keeping the commandments is as plain as the first. A person does NOT keep the commandments to be SAVED but does do so to get his prayers answered.

*1 John 3:22 And whatsoever we ask, we receive of him, because we **keep his commandments**, and do those things that are pleasing in his sight. 23 And this is **his commandment**, That we should believe on the name of his Son Jesus Christ, and love one another, as he gave us commandment. 24 And he that keepeth his commandments dwelleth in him, and he in him. And hereby we know that he abideth in us, by the Spirit which he hath given us.*

Read the first verse above again: *"keep the commandments"*—Why? The individual desires a particular outcome: to receive answered prayer. Verse 23 narrows down the range of *"his commandment"*—believe on Christ and love one another.

Verse 24 says that the indwelling Spirit testifies that Christ dwells within believers *(Romans 8:16)*. The Spirit bears witness, but this does not mean that believers cannot grieve or quench the Spirit *(Ephesians 4:30; 1 Thessalonians 5:19)*. The believers' failure to live right and do right has *hindered* many prayers.

*1 Peter 3:7 Likewise, ye husbands, dwell with them according to knowledge, giving honour unto the wife, as unto the weaker vessel, and as being heirs together of the grace of life; that your **prayers be not hindered**.*

Keep the Commandments of God: To Show you Love God

John and First John are complementary books. Both teach that believers keep biblical commandments to display their love of God outwardly. God NEVER told anyone, "If you want to gain eternal salvation, keep my commandments." NEVER! Not once! The Bible says:

*John 14:15 If ye love me, **keep my commandments.***

Sometimes truths are so simple they are missed. Here is a simple truth taught in the Bible: if you love God, keep the sayings (commandments) of God. In other words, doing what God says testifies to one's true love for Him. The disobedient simply do not love Him.

Nehemiah, while in captivity for the nation's disobedience, expressed his understanding of the ramifications of the Law when he confessed to God that the Jews had *"not kept the commandments" (Nehemiah 1:7)*. He pointed out that their refusal to keep the commandments caused their scattering around the world, and only obedience would enable their re-gathering *(Nehemiah 1:8-9)*.

In the New Testament, Paul described his blamelessness in the Law along with his Jewish legal pedigree. He also pointed out that keeping the Law was merely placing confidence in and trusting the flesh *(**Philippians 3:3-9**)*. Even adding good works to one's faith, why would anyone teach that trusting in one's flesh can save a soul?

*John 14:21 **He that hath my commandments, and keepeth them, he it is that loveth me**: and he that loveth me shall be loved of my Father, and I will love him, and will manifest myself to him. 22 Judas saith unto him, not Iscariot, Lord, how is it that thou wilt manifest* *thyself unto us, and not unto the world?* 23 *Jesus answered and said unto him, If a man love me, he will* **keep my words**: *and my Father will love him, and we will come unto him, and make our abode with him.* 24 *He that loveth me not* **keepeth not my sayings**: *and the word which ye hear is not mine, but the Father's which sent me.*

The contrast found within the verses concerns those who see the manifestation of God, something the world cannot see. God's demonstration of Himself only happens to those who love God.

Unfortunately, Bible teachers are becoming ever more guilty of forcing the Bible to say something it does not teach in an attempt to bolster their pet doctrines. Equating salvation to keeping the commandments is simply another of the private interpretations that have condemned and will condemn souls to Hell.

Keep the Commandments of God: To Testify of a Relationship with God

The book of Revelation points to those targeted for persecution by Satan. The persecuted (the remnant of the woman—Israel) have the testimony that they *"keep the commandments of God, and have the testimony of Jesus Christ."* This description of the believers testifies that they do what God tells them to do.

Revelation 12:17 *And the dragon was wroth with the woman, and went to make war with the remnant of* **her seed, which keep the commandments of God, and have the testimony of Jesus Christ**.

How can anyone sincerely pontificate that keeping the commandments of God plays a part in anyone's salvation? NOTHING within the context (or within the Bible) indicates that anyone keeps God's commandments to aid in salvation. Two chapters later Revelation reiterates this truth.

Revelation 14:12 *Here is the patience* **of the saints**: *here are they that* **keep the commandments of God, and the faith of Jesus**.

The saints during Daniel's Seventieth Week: 1) KEEP the commandments of God and 2) HAVE *"the faith of Jesus."* These two truths run parallel to **Galatians 2:20**. Galatians states that believers in the Church Age *"live by the faith the Son of God."*

***Galatians 2:20** I am crucified with Christ: nevertheless I live; yet not I, but Christ liveth in me: and the life which I now live in the flesh **I live by the faith of the Son of God**, who loved me, and gave himself for me.*

The saints in Revelation are obviously not rejecters of Jesus Christ, but spiritual brethren that have trusted in His salvation. They are saved by putting faith in the blood shed on the cross of Calvary. Any other means of salvation post-Calvary makes Christ's sacrifice pointless. Any teaching extolling the virtues of man's good works for salvation is heresy.

WARNING: Unfortunately, some of the most egregious Church Age teachings will outlast the Rapture. Those preaching during the Church Age, addressing the means and mode of salvation after the Rapture, will either help those living during Daniel's Seventieth Week or condemn them through their false teachings.

If a man preaches salvation by faith-plus-works and salvation is *not* by faith-plus-works, then these teachings become instruments of deception and channels of condemnation.

***Revelation 16:6** For they have shed the blood of **saints and prophets**, and thou hast given them blood to drink; for they are worthy.*

Saints and prophets will be persecuted and killed by Mark bearers and worshippers of the Beast.[3] If no one earns salvation through faith-plus-works after the Rapture, then those teaching this false doctrine must be thwarted. If salvation post-Rapture is in fact by grace through faith, then this truth must be taught without apology or apprehension. The scripture backs up only one of these teachings and refutes the other. The false teaching is a soul-condemning assertion that must be soundly denounced as heretical. Imagine a Bible teacher proclaiming that Christ's blood post-Rapture loses its ability to save those who trust in Christ.

---

[3] For an extensive discussion on **Revelation 22:14** concerning those that *"do his commandments,"* see **One Book Rightly Divided: Prophetic Edition** written by Stauffer and Ray and published in 2018 (pages 488, 549, 553, 556). Chapter 36 is titled *"The Tree of Life"* (pages 545–558).

7
Who is a Believer?

DURING THE CHURCH Age, the Bible labels believers with many designations such as Christians or brethren (or sisters), the sons of God, etc. Once God attaches these labels to an individual, the believer NEVER surrenders the designation by choice or by force. In other words, once a person becomes a brother in Christ, he NEVER ceases to be one of the brethren. Although differences exist between the standing of Church Age believers *(Ephesians 2:6; Philippians 1:23)* and post-Rapture believers, many fundamental truths remain consistent. The believers who die during Daniel's Seventieth Week go to Heaven, not to Abaraham's Bosom in the heart of the earth *(Revelation 6:9-11; Revelation 7:9, 14)*.

During Daniel's Seventieth Week, the Bible repeatedly refers to believers as *"the saints"* like here in Revelation, chapter 13.

> *Revelation 13:7 And it was given unto him to make war with **the saints**, and to overcome them: and power was given him over all kindreds, and tongues, and nations.*

The *"saints"* are obviously *believers* since the Beast makes *"war with the saints"* which includes people from *"all kindreds, and tongues, and nations."* The Beast will be wroth with the *"woman"* (which consists of all Israel) but only makes war with the *remnant* of her seed.

In the previous chapter of Revelation, Michael casts Satan, and his angels to earth *(Revelation 12:9)* and God pronounces a *"Woe"* to the *"inhabiters of the earth."* Satan shows up with *"great wrath"* knowing he has *"but a short time" (Revelation 12:12)*. He is going to do everything he can to destroy the saints of God since he hates God and His children.

The Devil persecutes the saints because of their testimony as willingly obedient followers of Christ.

Distinguishing the Two Remnants

Revelation chapter 12 distinguishes between the *"woman"*—all Israel, Jacob's seed—and the *"remnant of her seed."* This remnant of the woman's seed includes only the followers of Jesus Christ who have His testimony and keep the commandments of God.[1]

> **Revelation 12:17** *And the dragon was* **wroth with the woman***, and went to make war with* **the remnant of her seed***, which keep the commandments of God, and have the testimony of Jesus Christ.*

It is this remnant of the woman's seed (the true believers) who keep the commandments of God and have the testimony of Jesus Christ. The scripture refers to them as a "remnant" because not every Jew believes during Daniel's Seventieth Week. This remnant is simply those who have trusted in the Saviour. The Bible identifies the unbelieving populace as those who *"repented not"* during this time **(Revelation 9:20, 16:9, 16:11)**.

---

[1] When the Bible refers to those who *"keep the commandments of God,"* it NEVER infers some form of sinless perfection, whether in the future, today, or in the past. Some of the most aggressive defenders of the faith-plus-works-setup camouflage their dishonesty by *attempting to link* true scriptural teachings with Calvinism. This acrimonious approach involves creating a false association with an unsavory group (Calvinism in this case) to distract the reader from the truth. This philosophy of "ministry" is one of Satan's favorite devices against the body of Christ and causes unneeded division **(Romans 16:17-18)**.

The Bible teaches that good works **FOLLOW** saving faith regardless of the devices used to try to disprove this truth. Where there exists no corresponding outward change from the inward conversion, there exists no salvation! However, the depth **and permanency** of the *outward changes* depend upon the convert's willingness to act upon his new relationship with his Saviour. Regardless of how long the surrendered life lasts after the new birth, there is **ALWAYS** an *initial* change. Those identified in Revelation as keeping the commandments of God are NOT *earning* their soul's salvation. The passage offers a *description* of the believers—not the *conditions* for their soul's salvation. Attempting to attribute the teachings of sinless perfection, Calvinism, or Lordship salvation to these truths reveals the spiritual infidelity of the teacher. The faith-plus-works position is indefensible so they must distract the believer using a smokescreen to hide their deceptive tactics.

The vital question (answered later) is: how does one become a "saint" during Daniel's Seventieth Week?[2] A person TODAY in the Church Age becomes a *saint* by trusting in Jesus Christ as Saviour by faith. The Bible repeatedly addresses believers as *"saints"* **(Romans 15:25-26; 2 Corinthians 13:13; Ephesians 4:12; Colossians 1:2)**. Revelation refers to the *"patience and the faith of the saints."*

> *Revelation 13:10 He that leadeth into captivity shall go into captivity: he that killeth with the sword must be killed with the sword. Here is the patience and the faith of the **saints**.*

Saints are believers who have trusted in the blood that Christ shed for them. Only believers are called 1) *fellowservants*, 2) *brethren* and 3) *saints* during Daniel's Seventieth Week. As is God's customary approach, He distinguishes between the saved and the lost even if only within the context of a single verse. Scriptural context consistently defines itself. For instance, consider these two groups: the saved *remnant* **(Revelation 11:13; Revelation 12:17)** and the lost *remnant* **(Revelation 19:21)**. Context determines which remnant—either saved or lost.

> *Revelation 19:21 And **the remnant were slain** with the sword of him that sat upon the horse, which sword proceeded out of his mouth: and all the fowls were filled with their flesh.*

Take note of how this passage refers to a *lost "remnant"* who are NOT gathered when Christ sends His angels to gather the elect. When the Lord Jesus Christ returns on His white horse, He slays this lost *"remnant,"* while gathering those that are His.

> *Matthew 24:31 And he shall **send his angels** with a great sound of a trumpet, and they shall **gather together his elect** from the four winds, from one end of heaven to the other.*

The elect are the *"children of God"* whom God has redeemed **(1 John 3:10)**. Just like their Church Age counterparts, they become God's

---

[2] The cults teach that an individual must die in a "state of grace" to go to Heaven. Unfortunately, some "Bible-believers" inadvertently teach this same philosophy. Anyone asserting salvation by faith-plus-works ultimately teaches that souls must balance the judicial scales by life's end **(Matthew 24:13)**. Just because they do not believe the sacraments confer a "state of grace" does not make the teaching any more palatable or scriptural. They are blind leaders of the blind because they refuse to allow the scripture to be their final authority.

children through faith in Christ Jesus *(Galatians 3:26)*. The Bible also makes clear that children of the flesh (Jews by birth) are not the children of God *(Romans 9:8)*.

What is the destination of *brethren* at death after the Rapture during the "Tribulation"? According to scripture, John wrote that he saw *"under the altar" "the souls of them that were slain for the word of God" (Revelation 6:9)*. They were crying out for vengeance and told to wait for the killing of their fellowservants and brethren. White robes were given to everyone of them *(Revelation 6:11)*.

The hyperdispensationalist claims that those who *"die in the Lord" (Revelation 14:13)* after the Rapture go to a different destination after death. This teaching is nothing less than another private interpretation and additional wresting of the scripture. What saith the scripture concerning the destination of those who *"came out of great tribulation"* through death?

> **Revelation 7:9** *After this I beheld, and, lo,* **a great multitude**, *which no man could number, of all nations, and kindreds, and people, and tongues,* **stood before the throne, and before the Lamb**, *clothed with white robes, and palms in their hands;*

Something is amiss with the false interpretation that this great multitude standing before the throne and the Lamb is anywhere other than in Heaven. The raptured saints and these believers during Daniel's Seventieth Week are there together. When a believer dies after the Rapture, he departs to be with Christ which is far better than the situation he found himself while upon the earth.

8
Self-Defense Prohibited?

CONSIDER THE CONTEXT of Revelation, chapter 13. Amid the narrative of Daniel's Seventieth Week, a thought-provoking shift of focus takes place.

> **Revelation 13:10** He that leadeth into captivity shall go into captivity: **he that killeth with the sword must be killed with the sword.** Here is the patience and the faith of the saints.

The verse states those who kill must likewise be killed. A literal reading indicates that self-defense for believers (the saints) might be counter-productive and possibly prohibited during Daniel's Seventieth Week. This scriptural guidance runs contrary to man's instinct of self-preservation. Every saint needs patience and faith, especially if instructed not to put up a fight against Satan's worst onslaught.

No Self-defense Allowed

The Lord made a similar statement to His earthly disciples. As Judas and the soldiers were coming to arrest Jesus, He expressly prohibited them from defending themselves.

> **Matthew 26:52** Then said Jesus unto him, **Put up again thy sword into his place: for all they that take the sword shall perish with the sword.** 53 Thinkest thou that I cannot now pray to my Father, and he shall presently give me more than **twelve legions of angels**? 54 But how then shall the scriptures be fulfilled, that thus it must be?

This passage juxtaposes man's attempt to defend himself with God's infinite power of supernatural protection **(Isaiah 49:25-26)**. Twelve legions of angels certainly have sufficient power to protect. False post-tribulation rapturists who fault pre-tribulation rapture teachers for not teaching self-preservation techniques overlook this point. The only preparation anyone needs (although a moot point for the raptured Church) is instructions on how to *"draw nigh unto God" (James 4:8)*. Why not teach people to trust in God's provision and protection rather than promoting an impotent God *(Proverbs 21:31)*?

The Bible proves that those with the best chance of enduring Daniel's Seventieth Week are *not* the preppers with their stocked-piled supplies. Survival will *not* be based upon individual or collective marksmanship, nor skilled survivalist techniques. The best chance and ONLY hope for surviving rests with those TRUSTING IN THE LORD. These are the only ones who will *physically* endure unto the end *(Matthew 24:13)*.[1] The scripture attests to this fact in Mark chapter 13.

> **Mark 13:13 *And ye shall be hated of all men for my name's sake: but he that shall endure unto the end, the same shall be saved*.**

Those who ENDURE UNTO THE END are **physically** saved and will enter into the millennium with their natural bodies. They are the ones gathered by the angels for protection before Christ's return.

> ***Matthew 24:31** And he shall send **his angels** with a great sound of a trumpet, and they **shall gather together** his elect from the four winds, from one end of heaven to the other.*

Enduring unto the end means believers survived until the end of the seven years without being captured and killed. A feat only accomplished by faith in the Almighty, not by human ingenuity!

Revelation *seems to teach* a type of passive martyrdom—but certainly not salvation through some kind of works. The Bible addresses the saints of Daniel's Seventieth Week, stating that *"he that killeth with*

---

[1] The context of those who *"endure unto the end"* to be saved in **Matthew 24:13** is obviously PHYSICAL in nature given the context explicitly defined nine verses later. *"And except those days should be shortened, there should **no flesh** be saved: but for the elect's sake those days shall be shortened" **(Matthew 24:22)**.* Those believers who *"endure unto the end"* comprise the group that does not get caught and killed. They endure in faith and endure in physical suffering and tribulation. Thus, those who *"endure unto the end"* of the seven years are the ones that enter the millennium with natural bodies. However, those who teach a faith-plus-works-setup refuse to allow the Bible to define biblical terminology because their agenda trumps their expressed belief in the Bible. Not all so-called Bible-believers believe all the Bible.

*the sword must be killed with the sword" **(Revelation 13:10)***. Seems like an odd admonition if *"endure unto the end" **(Matthew 24:13)*** earns one spiritual salvation—which it does not!

The phrase *"take the sword shall perish with the sword"* implies that armed resistance or any type of "believers' militia" might be anti-scriptural. This kind of self-reliance during the time of Jacob's trouble is against the will of God. God supernaturally intervenes in unimaginable ways with strength and resilience on the believer's behalf during this time.

> ***Revelation 14:12** Here is the patience of the **saints**: here are they that **keep the commandments of God**, and the faith of Jesus. 13 And I heard a voice from heaven saying unto me, Write, **Blessed** are the dead which **die in the Lord** from henceforth: Yea, saith the Spirit, that they may rest from their labours; and their works do follow them.*

Interestingly, Revelation also mentions that the saints are *"blessed"* who *"die in the Lord."* The question must first be asked and then answered how a person *gets "in the Lord"* during that time. Today, a person must make a conscious decision to *believe "in the Lord" **(Acts 9:42)***; that believer is part of the brethren *"in the Lord" **(Philippians 1:14)*** and fellowservants *"in the Lord" **(Colossians 4:7)***. The same conscious choice to *believe* in the Lord in the future and *place one's faith* in the Lord puts that individual *"in the Lord."* This decision *of faith* does not end with the Church Age. However, hyper-dividing the Bible turns this truth of God into a lie.

Lordship Salvation: Surprise, Surprise

An individual during Daniel's Seventieth Week will need to make a deliberate choice to believe and thus become a saint. Those who teach "tribulation saints" must add works to their faith for salvation are unwittingly propagating the false teaching of Lordship salvation. This false teaching claims that the saint must *"endure"* by making Jesus Lord over everything lest he loses his salvation. The most extreme proponents of faith-plus-works salvation believe that a person must live an *almost perfect life* to keep his salvation. Unbelievable!

Daniel chapter 11 mentions the abomination of desolation *(Daniel 11:31)* which aligns with the statements of **Matthew 24:15**. Jesus tells those living in Jerusalem and Judea at that time when they witness this abomination to *"flee into the mountains"* and take *"flight" (Matthew 24:20)*. He does *not* tell them to stay and fight! God promises those who *"know their God"* strength and the ability to live heroically.

> **Daniel 11:32** *And such as do wickedly against the covenant shall he corrupt by flatteries: but* **the people that do know their God** *shall be strong, and do exploits.*

The Old Testament historical record offers an interesting perspective on God's past deliverance. Samuel told the nation of Israel that God *"himself saved you out of all your adversities and your tribulations" (1 Samuel 10:19)*. God is not going to leave believers to fend for themselves in Daniel's Seventieth Week. The only hope for "Tribulation" believers: Trust God!

> **Daniel 8:24** *And his power shall be mighty, but not by his own power: and he shall destroy wonderfully, and shall prosper, and practise, and shall* **destroy the mighty and the holy people**.

The LORD delivered in the past, delivers in the present, and will deliver in the future also. Yet, believers are not all promised a physical deliverance; many of them will be *"blessed"* to *"die in the Lord" (Revelation 14:13)*.

Olivet Discourse Prophecies

Matthew, chapter 24 and Mark, chapter 13 contain two of the accounts of Christ's Olivet Discourse. The Olivet Discourse offers pertinent details of the prophecies of Israel's Last Days and Christ's Second Coming to earth.

> **Matthew 24:23** *Then if any man shall say unto you, Lo, here is Christ, or there; believe it not.* 24 *For there shall arise false Christs, and false prophets, and shall shew great signs and wonders; insomuch that,* **if it were possible, they shall deceive the very elect.**

Within these teachings, Christ boldly declared that the saints of God would be protected from deception. Believers captured by Satan's minions have nothing to fear.

2 Timothy 1:7 *For God hath not given us the **spirit of fear**; but of power, and of love, and of a sound mind.* [2]

Yet, the faith-plus-works proponents simply overlook (or purposely reject) God's involvement in the lives of believers following the Church's Rapture.

Far too many of these false teachers cloak their opinions in so-called sound Bible teaching. Their opinions are nothing more than a reckless disregard for the truth. Some Bible teachers assert those living during Daniel's Seventieth Week succumb to the immense pressures of watching loved ones decapitated. They teach that believers will beg for their children's lives by willingly selling their souls for a morsel of bread or the "right" to buy and sell. Although these concepts seem plausible, they disregard God's promised assurances of supernatural intervention.

Surely, God can, and God will be able to feed the believing brethren hiding from the Beast! "Tribulation" saints will lack the natural means to care for themselves and their hungry families. This time is like no other ever faced by man and God uses extraordinary measures to protect His saints. **If you are ONE OF THOSE STILL Here at that time READING THIS BOOKLET, do not FALL FOR the DECEPTION that you must sell your soul and take the Mark to care for your family**. Trust in the LORD! He has always been and will always be sufficient to save those who trust in Him. There is nothing that the Devil can do to you or your love ones that God cannot overcome.

Whenever man's thoughts and teachings run contrary to the Bible, reject those teachings. Simply choose to refuse these manmade philosophies and seek the truth. When teachers make Christ-diminishing hypotheses and assumptions, does God cease to be the Almighty? What saith the scripture?

1 John 4:4 *Ye are of God, little children, and have overcome them: because **greater is he that is in you, than he that is in the world**.*

How can anyone who believes in the power of God today, reject teachings extolling the omnipotence of the same God during Daniel's

---

[2] Some hyper-dispensationalists claim ***2 Timothy 1:7*** cannot apply outside the Church Age because Paul wrote it "for the Church Age." This teaching is unfortunately short-sighted and reduces God to something He is not—inconsistent ***(Malachi 3:6; Hebrews 13:8)***.

Seventieth Week?[3] The indwelling God is far superior to all the devils in the world, including the Anti-Christ himself. Read God's directive and promise concerning those delivered up for refusing to take the Mark of the Beast. God provides for every need!

> ***Mark 13:11** But **when they shall** lead you, and **deliver you up**, take no thought beforehand what ye shall speak, neither do ye premeditate: but whatsoever shall be given you in that hour, that speak ye: **for it is not ye that speak, but the Holy Ghost**.*

The Holy Ghost intervenes on behalf of believers *(Jeremiah 15:21)*. Satan's servants will compel many to take the Mark, but mere coercion cannot overcome God's supernatural protection (except for those who believe in the impotent God of the Hyperdispensationalists). Those arrested during Daniel's Seventieth Week and prosecuted are required to recant their faith and bow the knee to the image.

These captives are not the first to refuse to serve false gods and worship a golden image. The three Jewish captives in Daniel chapter 3 refused to bow to the image. Shadrach, Meshach, and Abendnego reveal how God likely intervenes on behalf of those compelled by the Antichrist. Their words are not their own but God-given.

> ***Daniel 3:16** Shadrach, Meshach, and Abed-nego, answered and said to the king, O Nebuchadnezzar, **we are not careful to answer** thee in this matter. 17 If it be so, our God whom we serve is able to deliver us from the burning fiery furnace, and he will deliver us out of thine hand, O king. 18 But if not, be it known unto thee, O king, that we will not serve thy gods, nor worship the golden image which thou hast set up.*

The believers refuse to comply. Their words will be God-ordained. Unlike these three Hebrew young men, many or all of them, will take their place in the hall of martyrs for the faith of Jesus Christ for whom they died.

---

[3] The hyper-dispensationalist who hyper-divides Hebrews through Revelation into "Tribulation" books might try to divide this verse back into a Church Age application. Such predictability is the pinnacle of hypocrisy and inconsistency clothed in a false spirituality. If First John is a "Tribulation" epistle (as they claim), the verse says that God is in the believers providing the power to overcome the world. Again, salvation is 100% dependent upon God.

***Revelation 20:4** And I saw thrones, and they sat upon them, and judgment was given unto them: and I saw **the souls of them that were beheaded** for the witness of Jesus, and for the word of God, and **which had not worshipped the beast, neither his image, neither had received his mark** upon their foreheads, or in their hands; and they lived and reigned with Christ a thousand years.*

Those Killed Awaiting the Death of Their Brethren

During the first half of Daniel's Seventieth Week, while Michael remains upon the earth, he serves as Israel's protector. At the midpoint, God summons Michael to Heaven to forcibly cast Satan to earth *(Revelation 12:7-9)*.[4] With Michael in Heaven after the midpoint of the seven years, he is no longer upon the earth to protect Israel. With Satan now bound to earth, he goes into the Temple of God and desecrates the Temple *(2 Thessalonians 2:4)*. At this point, Israel is told to flee at this abomination of desolation *(Matthew 24:15-18)*.

Interestingly, the saints who are slain for the word of God and the testimony (of Jesus) during Daniel's Seventieth Week appear under the altar. They want to know when God's vengeance will be poured out upon their persecutors and executioners.

---

[4] IMAGINE if Satan's last "hurrah" (or so he thinks) will take place as all believers *"stand before the judgment seat of Christ" **(Romans 14:10)***. This Judgment Seat takes place AFTER the Rapture but before the midpoint of Daniel's Seventieth Week. At this time, Satan still has access to God in Heaven *(Job 1:6, Job 2:1)*. As Christians stand in judgment for their work *(1 Corinthians 3:13)*, what better opportunity for the prideful accuser of the brethren to hurl his baseless accusations against the redeemed *(1 Peter 1:18-19)*? Christians will need their Advocate more than at any other time in man's history. An advocate is *"one who defends, vindicates, or espouses a cause, by argument."*

There is no better time to *"have an advocate with the Father" **(1 John 2:1)*** who can and will shoot down every accusation made by *"the accuser of our brethren" **(Revelation 12:10)***. That Advocate is *"Jesus Christ the righteous"* who needs only to point to His five wounds to plead the blood in the believer's defense. The Judgment Seat of Christ is a time for the Christian's accountability for the work done or the work squandered, not a time of punishment or purgatory.

Following Christ's thumping of Satan in this heavenly judicial tribunal, Michael will be called upon to cast Satan out of Heaven. Revelation then expresses a *"Woe to the inhabiters of earth"* because the Devil will know that *"he hath but a short time" **(Revelation 12:12)***.

***Revelation 6:9** And when he had opened the fifth seal, I saw under the altar the souls of them that were **slain for the word of God, and for the testimony which they held**: 10 And they cried with a loud voice, saying, How long, O Lord, holy and true, dost thou not judge and avenge our blood on them that dwell on the earth? 11 And white robes were given unto every one of them; and it was said unto them, that they should **rest** yet for a little season, **until their fellowservants also and their brethren, that should be killed as they were, should be fulfilled**.*

God tells the saints killed during Daniel's Seventieth Week to wait until their "fellowservants" and "brethren" are also killed. Only then will God take out His vengeance upon the earth's unbelieving populace. God does not tell these martyred saints to wait until the Rapture (that has already taken place several years earlier); the Lord says to wait until their fellow-brethren (the other believers) are KILLED. While those under the altar are awaiting their brethren's death, the brethren on earth are awaiting Christ's return to gather them.[5]

Christ's return at the end of the seven years with His armies in ***Revelation 19:11-14*** will be to gather the elect for protection ***(Matthew 24:11)*** while He administers His wrath and vengeance upon the unbelievers ***(Revelation 19:15; 2 Thessalonians 1:7-10)***.

---

[5] Those referred to as *"brethren"* during Daniel's Seventieth Week (***Revelation 6:10, 12:10***) should not be confused with those called *brethren* during Christ's ministry ***(Matthew 28:10; John 20:17)***. **Spiritual** brethren through their relationship with Christ are transformed through the blood. **Physical** brethren (Jews by birth) who never become spiritual brethren (saved) remain lost regardless of dispensation. Those who assert that God accepts Christ-rejecting Jews in any dispensation are simply duped into believing another of the heresies perpetrated by Satan. The *brethren* referenced in Revelation during Daniel's Seventieth Week are spiritual brethren through the new birth not physical brethren.

9
The Deceived Take the Mark

GOD SOMETIMES ALLOWS Bible truths to remain buried until He gives the insights needed to excavate them *(Proverbs 25:2)*. For instance, the narrative of Christ's return to earth at the Second Coming *(Revelation 19:11)* contains the critical component concerning those who ultimately receive the Mark of the Beast. This truth offers some significant insights into the specifics of who CAN and who CANNOT take the Mark and worship his image.

> *Revelation 19:20 And the beast was taken, and with him the false prophet that wrought miracles before him, with **which he deceived them that had received the mark of the beast, and them that worshipped his image**. These both were cast alive into a lake of fire burning with brimstone.*

Notice the group specified as subject to the Beast's blasphemous idolatry—only the DECEIVED are subject to taking the Mark! **God supernaturally protects BELIEVERS from THIS deception, WHICH PROTECTS THEM from taking the Mark.** (Reread this point until this truth sinks in!) God protects believers from deception, which protects their souls from damnation. A man's salvation is dependent upon God's supernatural interventions, not upon man's capabilities to withstand coercion and force.

The Mark of the Beast serves as the seal and authorization for the followers of the Antichrist. People must accept this Mark to buy or sell *(Revelation 13:15-18, 14:11, 15:2, 16:2, 19:20, 20:4)*. The False Prophet (or Second Beast) induces people through deceptive means to take the Mark and worship the First Beast. The Mark is placed IN the hand or IN and UPON the forehead, which could indicate a biometric computer chip.

This deception revolves around making man believe that he is the true Christ *(Matthew 24:23)*, whether through raising the dead *(Revela-*

tion 13:3-4) or instituting a false system of worship *(Revelation 13:12)*, the goal is deception. He also deceives through making real fire come down from heaven *(Revelation 13:13)*. The ultimate outcome of it all: deceive the inhabitants of earth.

> **Revelation 13:14 And deceiveth them that dwell on the earth by the means of those miracles which he had power to do in the sight of the beast**; *saying to them that dwell on the earth, that they should make an image to the beast, which had the wound by a sword, and did live.*

Supernatural Protection from the Mark

Those who take the Mark willingly CHOOSE to do so. They are DECEIVED into receiving it and DECEIVED into worshipping the image of the Beast.[1] One of those deceptions involves accepting Satan's offer for buying and selling *(Revelation 13:17)* and rejecting God's ever-present supernatural protection for those who choose to trust in His supernatural provisions.

The Bible says the False Prophet *"**deceived them** that had received the mark of the beast."* Those deceived by the miracles of the False Prophet are the ONLY ones who will receive the Mark. Plain and simple! The two rules: no deception/no Mark; no supernatural protection/deception and Mark. Here is the verse again:

> **Revelation 19:20** *And the beast was taken, and with him the false prophet that* **wrought miracles before** *him, with* **which he deceived them that had received the mark of the beast, and them that worshipped his image**. *These both were cast alive into a lake of fire burning with brimstone.*

This truth is straightforward and easily comprehended; however, it is important to take note of the reason for the PAST TENSE nature of the passage. The description found in verse 20 follows Christ's return in verse 11 serving to **recount** the miracles, the deception, the receiving

---

[1] From the very beginning, deception has been an essential element of Satan's modus operandi: *"And Adam was not deceived, but **the woman being <u>deceived</u>** was in the transgression" **(1 Timothy 2:14)**.* Eve ate of the forbidden fruit because she chose the satanic deception over God's supernatural provision and protection. God could have protected Adam and Eve from the deception and Eve would never have succumbed. Without the Lord's protection from the deception, the believers during Daniel's Seventieth Week will have no power to withstand *(Matthew 24:24)*.

of the Mark and the worshipping of the Beast's image during Daniel's Seventieth Week.

This passage serves as a historical examination—not an ongoing narrative as the events transpire. **The verse points out again that the deception precedes taking the Mark and worshipping the image.** The Beast will deceive and convince the non-believers that they must take the Mark and worship the Beast to survive.

The Beast will use *"great wonders"* and other miracles, like causing fire to come down from heaven and giving life to the image as a means to DECEIVE. Yet, those who are NOT DECEIVED by these wonders will NOT take the Mark and worship the beast, thus subjecting them to execution if captured.

> *Revelation 13:11 And I beheld another beast coming up out of the earth; and he had two horns like a lamb, and he spake as a dragon. 12 And he exerciseth all the power of the first beast before him, and causeth the earth and them which dwell therein to worship the first beast, whose deadly wound was healed. 13 And he doeth great wonders, so that he maketh fire come down from heaven on the earth in the sight of men, 14* ***And deceiveth them that dwell on the earth by the means of those miracles*** *which he had power to do in the sight of the beast; saying to them that dwell on the earth, that they should make an image to the beast, which had the wound by a sword, and did live. 15 And he had power to give life unto the image of the beast, that the image of the beast should both speak,* ***and cause that as many as would not worship the image of the beast should be killed.***

According to the Beast's statutes forced upon mankind, no one can buy or sell without the Mark *(Revelation 13:16-18)*. This fact does not preclude God from supernaturally providing sustenance to His saints who refuse the Mark. God has historically provided manna from Heaven. It is spiritual infidelity to ignore this fact and teach that man must survive without God during the most tumultuous time in man's history.

The God of the present and the God of the past is the same God of the future. For forty years in the wilderness, God provided food for millions *(Exodus 16:35)*. The same God multiplied five loaves and two fishes to feed five thousand men *(Matthew 14:19-21)*. Even after the Church Age has ended, God can, and God will supernaturally and continuously protect His own *(Matthew 24:22; Revelation 12:16)*.

The passage from Revelation chapter 13 reveals WHY *unbelievers* take the Mark—they are DECEIVED into receiving it. This point cannot be overemphasized; it bears repeating one more time—only the DECEIVED are going to take the Mark and only the DECEIVED worship the Beast. *Believers* who need food to survive are NOT going to take the Mark to satisfy the flesh since they have a supernatural Protector and Provider in their Saviour. Those teaching that man trusting in self has the best chance to survive condemns souls that believe their lies.

Warnings Against Deception

The Lord addressed Daniel's Seventieth Week during His Olivet discourse. He repeatedly warned of the heightened time of deception during this period. Discernment will be critical to those susceptible to the deception. Christ's warning was simple: Do not be DECEIVED; many (including false prophets) will DECEIVE many.

> *Matthew 24:4 And Jesus answered and said unto them,* **Take heed that no man deceive you***.*
>
> *Matthew 24:5 For* **many** *shall come in my name, saying, I am Christ; and* **shall deceive many***.*
>
> *Matthew 24:11 And* **many false prophets** *shall rise, and* **shall deceive many***.*

Christ's repeated warnings during the Olivet discourse concerning succumbing to deception are not coincidental. Heeding this warning is the difference between eternal life and eternal damnation.[2] God saves sinners that come to Him of their own free will and rejects no one that willingly trusts in Him.

Faith and trust in God will remain the means whereby one pleases God in the future Age *(Hebrews 11:6)*. In the Old Testament, Isaiah referred to man's *"righteousnesses"* as filthy rags; time has reinforced this truth throughout every Age *(Isaiah 64:6)*. Christ died for the iniquity of every sinner—past, present, and future *(Isaiah 53:6; Philippians 3:9)*.

---

[2] The Calvinist teaching claims that those born blind *(2 Corinthians 4:3-4)* are incapable of trusting God, but this is a false manmade doctrine. False teachings are the greatest hindrances to putting all the spiritual pieces of the puzzle together. Until the sinner trusts in the Saviour for salvation, he will be susceptible to deception. Once he trusts in the blood shed for him, he will *"abide under the shadow of the Almighty" (Psalm 91:1)*.

This truth remains the "formula" for salvation even during Daniel's Seventieth Week—receive Christ by faith! Reject Him and be deceived.

Throughout Christ's earthly ministry, Jesus promised to give His sheep eternal life *(John 10:27-28)* and stated that *"they shall never perish, neither shall any man pluck them out of my hand."* It is impossible to invalidate a believer's salvation once a person has trusted in the Lord; he is eternally secure.

God CAN impart this same level of assurance of salvation toward those who have trusted in Him FOLLOWING the Rapture DURING Daniel's Seventieth Week. Of course, it is possible *(Matthew 19:25-26)*! The question is *"What saith the scripture?"*

God's Protection from Deception

The believer does not need to rely upon his own futile attempts to withstand soul-condemning temptation. During this period of amplified deception, man's ONLY hope of withstanding the deception will be trusting in the Almighty.

Consider the last chapter of the book of Hebrews. In the context of God's eternal promises, the passage contains both an admonition not to fear what man shall do AND a promise that God will NOT forsake the believer.[3]

---

[3] With the clear promise of eternal security found within the book of Hebrews *(i.e. Hebrews 13:5-6)*, it is hard to imagine how any Bible-believer could justify teaching that Hebrews communicates the loss of salvation THROUGHOUT the book. Does the Bible contain contradictions? Certainly not! Yet, the hyper-dispensationalist ignores verses like these and chooses to point to their private interpretations of Hebrews chapters 3, 6, and 10 as supposed justification for ignoring Hebrews chapter 13 and elsewhere. Why do they ignore this truth? Because exalting dogmatic assertions over the plain teachings of scripture aligns them with their peers for whom they seek approbation and esteem. They would rather create a smokescreen between their teachings and the truth, thus disregarding that all scripture is profitable AND DOCTRINAL *(1 Timothy 3:16)*.

The truth is plain and it is straightforward: Hebrews contains eternal security passages applicable for the believer. Yet, the spiritual infidelity of the most ardent Bible critics compel them to ignore this truth. Instead, they believe that the book of Hebrews teaches that God will NOT save the sinner nor keep the saved sinner saved without him working to stay saved. Blasphemy! This false ideology forces an unreal scenario. Future believers are to reject Hebrews chapter 13 because it supposedly does not apply to them although the hyper-dispensationalist claims that the rest of the book is addressed TO those in the "Tribulation." In other words, this promise must be

> **Hebrews 13:5** *Let your conversation be without covetousness; and be content with such things as ye have:* **for he hath said, I will never leave thee, nor forsake thee.** *6 So that we may boldly say, **The Lord is my helper, and I will not fear what man shall do unto me**.*

During Daniel's Seventieth Week, the saints/brethren/fellowservants are those who have trusted in the Lord. **They are supernaturally protected from the satanic miracles and devilish deception.** Supernatural protection means that the elect are *no longer* vulnerable and hence cannot be deceived **into believing the miracles** that the Anti-Christ performs.

The synoptic gospels (Matthew, Mark and Luke) offer the best narrative concerning the attempts at this satanic deception.

Several times Matthew refers to the believers of Daniel's Seventieth Week as the elect. When Matthew refers to the believing Jews as the *elect*, it is essential to understand that the elect become the elect at salvation when God elects them (and not before that time).[4] It is also important to note that these three gospel books do not refer to believers as "saints," "brethren" or "fellowservants" (like Revelation) but only as the *"elect."* Each designation refers to the same group—the redeemed.

Matthew associates the shortening of the days to the preservation of the elect. God shortens the days, not to *save the souls* of the elect (which souls He has already saved) but to save flesh (physical life). Otherwise, no one could survive Satan's dreadful onslaught.

> **Matthew 24:22** *And except those days should be shortened, there should **no flesh be saved**: but **for the elect's sake** those days shall be shortened.*

Matthew also points out that the angels sent preceding Christ's return, gather only a select group—the elect. The following passage proves that the elect only includes the saved.

"rightly divided" away from those in Daniel's Seventieth Week! A shameful tactic at best! A sinful soul-condemning achievement at worst!

[4] Understanding how someone becomes a part of the "elect" is quite simple to grasp by relating the truths to something already familiar. Political elections offer a good parallel. When does a candidate for office become the elect? He becomes the elect AFTER the election once he has been elected. The same principle applies to the Bible. When someone trusts in the Saviour, the individual becomes the elect but not before this time.

*Matthew 24:31 And he shall send his **angels** with a great sound of a trumpet, and they shall **gather together his elect** from the four winds, from one end of heaven to the other.*

Those gathered by the angels in advance of Christ's return to earth include ONLY believers—whether referred to as the *elect* in Matthew or the *saints, brethren,* and *fellowservants* in Revelation. Christ kills all those *NOT* gathered by the angels (the non-elect—unbelievers) **at His Second Coming.**

God's supernatural protection does *not* protect believers from being put to death but only from Satan's deception.

*Matthew 24:23 Then if any man shall say unto you, Lo, here is Christ, or there; believe it not. 24 For there shall arise false Christs, and false prophets, and shall shew great signs and wonders; insomuch that, **if it were possible, they shall deceive the very elect**.*

The signs and wonders during Daniel's Seventieth Week are so convincing that IF IT WERE POSSIBLE, these miracles would *"deceive the very elect."* This warning indicates that without God's merciful and gracious intervention, the believers (the elect) could not and would not withstand the deception.[5]

---

[5] Some of the most significant disagreements amongst Bible students concerns hermeneutics, especially when the dispute involves a novice of the scripture. These Bible apprentices are most vulnerable to allowing their preconceived notions to govern their understanding of fundamental Bible interpretation. This pitfall occurs in three primary areas: 1) grasping the basic application of the rules of grammar, 2) understanding that every usage of a Bible phrase (or word) does not necessarily imply the same interpretation or conclusion, and 3) recognizing that context ALWAYS determines the meaning of words and phrases.

Like the Alexandrian crowd, an obstinate hyper-dispensationalist always attempts to justify his unwarranted eisegesis of passages. This mindset causes him to swerve into the ditch on the opposite side of the proverbial highway. The context of the statement ("if it were possible") when referring to attempts to seduce the saints is a prime example. This phrase contextually concerns the need of God's supernatural intervention to make that which is *possible*, now *impossible* through supernatural intervention AS PROMISED ELSEWHERE *(Mark 13:10-11; Luke 21:12-15)*. This is where Bible study gets tricky for the spiritual rookie.

Contextually, this phrase when associated with the Lord's prayer requesting the Father's intervention in the Garden offers a different application. When the phrase, "If it were possible" or "If it be possible" is used as a prayer request *(Matthew 26:39)*, it differs from the use here. For instance, in the Garden, Jesus was requesting: *"If it BE* (or *"if it WERE") possible"* please change the inevitable outcome *(Matthew 26:39; Mark*

Hyper-dispensationalists by their teaching infer that the God of the Church Age somehow becomes impotent after the Rapture. Quite to the contrary, God's protective hand is THE ONLY HOPE of salvation and THE ONLY HOPE for security during the time of Jacob's Trouble *(Jeremiah 30:7)*. The same God that Christians serve today will remain active in the future. He can and will supernaturally provide for a believer's needs *(Philippians 4:19)*. To claim that God cannot or will not protect "Tribulation" believers is to call God a liar.

*Matthew 24:23 Then if any man shall say unto you, Lo, here is Christ, or there; **believe it not**.*

During Daniel's Seventieth Week, false teachers are proclaiming that Christ has returned. The Bible warns those in hiding to *"believe it not"* because when the Son of God (Christ) shows up every eye shall see Him *(Revelation 1:7)*.

The sister passage to **Matthew 24:24** indicates that the false Christs and false prophets attempt to use their signs and wonders *"to seduce"* those protected from satanic seduction.

*Mark 13:22 For false Christs and false prophets shall rise, and shall shew signs and wonders, to **seduce, if it were possible, even the elect**.*

The truth rejectors will refuse to trust in the name of the Lord to be saved (or delivered). No trust in the arm of flesh can withstand the deception. Man's only hope remains the power of an omnipotent God.

Fortunately, God offers a SECOND WITNESS in the books of Mark and Luke with additional details concerning the Olivet discourse. The

---

13:22). The Lord's prayer request should NOT be directly likened with the statement of fact, as seen in Matthew chapter 24 and elsewhere. Context determines meaning not forced uniformity by the novice.

The same application with varying connotations applies to the instances of this phrase ("If it were possible") that occur twice in the book of Acts. In these two instances, through the resultant actions of Paul, specific outcomes WOULD happen *(Acts 20:16; Acts 27:39)*. Unless Paul takes a certain course of action, the improbable (or impossible) will NOT come to pass. Paul determined to sail by Ephesus because failing to do so would make it impossible for him to make it to Jerusalem by Pentecost *(Acts 20:16)*. In these two cases, the context of this phrase is making the *impossible* now *possible*. This turns out to be just the opposite context of the subject verse. It is essential to recognize that context always determines the meaning of phrases. Yet, *the novice* unwittingly forces his private interpretation into the scripture because of his spiritual immaturity. Sad but quite common!

Olivet discourse recorded in three synoptic gospels provides a scenario of how believers are to react when they are captured and imprisoned. Carefully read these next two passages; God WILL supernaturally protect believers from denying Him.

> **Mark 13:10** *And the gospel must first be published among all nations. 11 But* **when they shall lead you, and deliver you up,** *take no thought beforehand what ye shall speak, neither do ye premeditate: but whatsoever shall be given you in that hour, that speak ye: for* **it is not ye that speak, but the Holy Ghost.**

> **Luke 21:12** *But before all these, they shall lay their hands on you, and persecute you,* **delivering you up to the synagogues, and into prisons***, being brought before kings and rulers for my name's sake. 13 And it shall turn to you for a testimony. 14* **Settle it therefore in your hearts, not to meditate before what ye shall answer:** *15* **For I will give you a mouth and wisdom,** *which all your adversaries shall not be able to gainsay nor resist.*

The Lord tells believers during Daniel's Seventieth Week NOT even to think about what they will say when captured. The *"patience of the saints"* will be their guide, and the words they speak will be the Lord's words. God is going to speak FOR them and THROUGH them. Deception brings sure damnation, but God protects those who trust in Him from the damnable deception. With God protecting believers, why would anyone teach that a believer must save himself through his works (plus faith) following the Rapture?

Second Thessalonians gives further insights by emphasizing the satanic signs and lying wonders. These deceptions are accepted *"in them that perish,"* NOT by believers whom God supernaturally protects.

> **2 Thessalonians 2:9** *Even him, whose coming is after the working of Satan with all power and signs and lying wonders, 10 And with all* **deceivableness** *of unrighteousness* **in them that perish***; because they received not the love of the truth, that they might be saved.*

Revelation further pinpoints those who perish, stating it is those whose names are *not* written the book of life **(Revelation 13:8; Revelation 17:8)**. No man has ever been capable of doing any amount of "good" work to save himself. Those who trust in self (and their works) will be hopelessly overwhelmed by Satan's deceptive tactics.

There are some preachers today who are falsely teaching that the **strong delusion** *(2 Thessalonians 2:11)* during Daniel's Seventieth Week is teaching that a person gets *saved by grace through faith without works* during that time. As with all falsehood, one erroneous teaching frequently leads to the most egregious of hypotheses. Very few positions have been as silly as this one, but once someone closes their mind to the truth, Satan has free reign.

Multitudes Saved Following the Rapture

Again, if you are reading this booklet after the Rapture of the Church, your ONLY hope will be to trust in the saving grace accessible only because of Christ's sacrifice on the cross. The blood of Christ remains the only sufficient payment to save your soul.

Yet, many pontificators of scripture claim that very few if any souls will be saved during Daniel's Seventieth Week. The Bible explicitly contradicts these thoughts. In fact, multitudes will be saved during Daniel's Seventieth Week as attested to in the next verse.

> ***Revelation 7:9*** *After this I beheld, and, lo,* ***a great multitude****, which no man could number, of all nations, and kindreds, and people, and tongues,* ***stood before the throne, and before the Lamb****, clothed with white robes, and palms in their hands;*

This mass of people who have been redeemed by the blood of the Lamb will stand before the Lamb who sits upon His throne. There is no need to guess concerning the identity of this great multitude, but when inquiry is made, the answer is simple and straightforward.

> ***Revelation 7:14*** *And I said unto him, Sir, thou knowest. And he said to me,* ***These are they which came out of great tribulation****, and have washed their robes, and made them white in the blood of the Lamb.*

This multitude standing before the throne of the Lamb in Heaven came out of *"great tribulation."* Their robes are white having been washed in the *"blood of the Lamb."* Multitudes will come to believe that JESUS STILL SAVES!

10
How are the Lost Saved?

CERTAIN GROUPS OF believers have hotly and raucously contested the question of how a person gets saved in the future. Yet, God always gives the sought-after answers to those that exalt the truth over all else. The chronology provided in Second Thessalonians chapter two provides an excellent place to show how someone gets saved during Daniel's Seventieth Week.

> *2 Thessalonians 2:1 Now we beseech you, brethren, by the coming of our Lord Jesus Christ, and by **our gathering together unto him** [**Rapture**], 2 That ye be not soon shaken in mind, or be troubled, neither by spirit, nor by word, nor by letter as from us, as that the day of Christ is at hand. 3 Let no man deceive you by any means: for that day shall not come, except there come a falling away first, and that man of sin be revealed, the son of perdition; 4 Who opposeth and exalteth himself above all that is called God, or that is worshipped; so that he **as God sitteth in the temple of God** [**Midpoint**], shewing himself that he is God.*

The chronology of Second Thessalonians chapter two is easily identified: **verse 1** begins with the Rapture (the Day of Christ), moving to the midpoint of the seven years in **verse 4** (the Abomination of Desolation), and onto the end of the seven years (the Second Coming) in **verse 8**. Read the next passage and see.

> *2 Thessalonians 2:8 And then shall that Wicked be revealed, whom the Lord shall consume with the spirit of his mouth, and shall destroy with the brightness of **his coming** [**Second Coming**]:*

With these three events pinpointed in the passage [Rapture, Midpoint, Second Coming], God reveals the chronology of the passage. This chapter covers all seven years and does so chronologically. As Second

Thessalonians starts with the Rapture (the gathering together), it mentions only ONE event that comes FIRST (before the Rapture)—the apostasy of believers.[1] The narrative then spans the entire seven-year period. Notice the wording of *verse 3*—the only thing that must chronologically take place FIRST (or before the Rapture) is the "falling away" or apostasy.

> *2 Thessalonians 2:3 Let no man deceive you by any means: for that day shall not come, except there come a falling away first,* **[then the chronology moves forward 3 ½ years]** *and that man of sin be revealed, the son of perdition;*

There is only one event mentioned as happening **FIRST** before the Rapture (not two, unless you change the Bible rearrange the words or ignore the context).

The events recorded in verses 10 through 12 (below) have nothing to do with the Church Age *(doctrinally)*. They do not directly reference the rejection of the gospel before the Rapture but may be *spiritually* applied to all. Many misteach this application by regurgitating what others taught them.

> *2 Thessalonians 2:10 And with all* **deceivableness of unrighteousness in them that perish**; *because they received not the love of the truth, that they might be* **saved**. *11 And for this cause* **God shall send them strong delusion**, *that they should believe a lie: 12 That they all might be* **damned who believed not the truth**, *but had pleasure in unrighteousness.*

Verse 9 points to the one who will come after the working of Satan—the Beast. He is the one who has deceived those who perish and comes *"with all* **deceivableness of unrighteousness**.*"* Why is the group addressed perishing? The Bible says they are perishing because *"they received not the love of the truth"* (during Daniel's Seventieth Week) THAT THEY MIGHT BE SAVED! That is the context and context does matter in Bible interpretation! Plain and simple: Those who reject the truth will be damned.

---

[1] See a lengthy discussion covering the matter in **"Reviving the Blessed Hope"** and **"When the End Begins"** available at **www.BibleDoug.com**.

Again, the Bible identifies the damned as those who perish. The damned refused to *believe* the truth. The context has nothing to do with those who failed to *"endure unto the end."*[2] The damned are deceived because they refused to be saved; this salvation is the ONLY God-ordained protection from deception. The signs and wonders of the false Christs and false prophets deceive *unbelievers*, but *believers* CANNOT be deceived by the false christs and false prophets **(Matthew 24:24)**.

Identifying the Strong Delusion (verse 11):

For decades, Bible teachers have pontificated what the Bible means when it says that *"God shall send them strong delusion."* Consider first a precedent when Satan attacked Job: God took personal responsibility for allowing Satan to move against Job *(Job 2:3)*. During Daniel's Seventieth Week, God is going to cast the great deceiver to earth who will then deceive earth's inhabitants—that is God's strong delusion. Delusions are rampant now but imagine how much worse it will be when Satan knows that he is bound to earth.

> **Revelation 12:9** And the **great dragon was cast out,** that old serpent, called the Devil, and Satan, **which deceiveth the whole world**: he was **cast out into the earth**, and his angels were cast out with him.

How will an individual at that time avoid the strong delusion? ONLY by faith in Jesus Christ! ONLY by coming under God's protective hand! Those present during Daniel's Seventieth Week will hear the gospel preached by the Two Witnesses, the 144,000 and the angel flying amid the first heaven with the Everlasting Gospel **(Revelation 14:6)**. Every in-

---

[2] *Enduring to the end* refers to the oft quoted verse from Matthew chapter 24. The hyper-dispensationalist takes the passage out of God's intended context to teach that a man must endure (or work or withstand) *temptation* until the end of his life to gain eternal life. This is a shameful twisting of scripture: *"But he that shall **endure unto the end**, the same shall be saved"* **(Matthew 24:13)**. This passage refers to those who endure (live) by not getting killed throughout the seven years thus entering the millennium alive. Those guilty of confusing others concerning this teaching should repent, understand the doctrine, and quit repeating this erroneous false teaching. Souls in the future who believe this false teaching of dying in a state of grace will be damned by believing the lie propagated today.

dividual must believe the truth to be saved, and only then will the strong delusion be powerless to persuade.[3]

The most important question of all: Does the Bible definitively point out how someone gets saved? Yes, in Acts chapter 2. This chapter records Peter preaching the events of Daniel's Seventieth Week. This Week of years includes Israel's last days, the prophecy, visions, dreams, wonders, signs, etc., culminating in the sun turned dark, and the moon turned into blood.

> *Acts 2:17 And it shall come to pass in the last days, saith God, I will pour out of my Spirit upon all flesh: and your sons and your daughters shall prophesy, and your young men shall see visions, and your old men shall dream dreams: 18 And on my servants and on my handmaidens I will pour out in those days of my Spirit; and they shall prophesy: 19 And I will shew wonders in heaven above, and signs in the earth beneath; blood, and fire, and vapour of smoke: 20* **The sun shall be turned into darkness, and the moon into blood,** *before that great and notable day of the Lord come:*

The context of this description matches the events surrounding the sixth seal when the moon is turned into blood **(Revelation 6:12)**. These events take place before Christ's Second Advent. Peter concludes his comments with the words indicating that God intends to be taken literally. The following reveals God's design for deliverance during Daniel's Seventieth Week:

> *Acts 2:21 And it shall come to pass, that* **whosoever shall call on the name of the Lord shall be saved**.

> *Joel 2:32 And it shall come to pass, that* **whosoever shall call on the name of the LORD shall be delivered**: *for in mount Zion and in Jerusalem shall be deliverance, as the LORD hath said, and in the remnant whom the LORD shall call.*

How does someone during Daniel's Seventieth Week get delivered from the onslaught of deception? According to Peter' preaching, deliv-

---

[3] According to the hyper-dispensationalist, part of the message in the future will be that grace will not save you; the blood of Christ is insufficient, and self-reliance is the key to salvation.

erance ONLY comes to those calling on the name of the Lord! They are to trust in the Lord.

- Whosoever shall call upon the name of the Lord is **saved**.
- Whosoever shall call upon the name of the Lord is a **saint**.
- Whosoever shall call upon the name of the Lord is one of the **brethren**.
- Whosoever shall call upon the name of the Lord is a **fellowservant**.

What about spiritual deliverance and salvation? This happens the same way; the individual must trust in the Lord. Only those who understand Christ's blood sacrifice trust in Him *(Revelation 12:11)*. When the individual calls on the name of the Lord, from that point forward, he has God's promise of supernatural protection from deception. Only those who trust in the Lord will call upon Him to be saved/delivered. God dwells in believers in the future just like today.

*1 John 4:4 Ye are of God, little children, and have overcome them: because **greater is he that is in you**, than he that is in the world.*

*1 John 4:13 Hereby know we that we **dwell** in him, and he **in us**, because he hath **given us of his Spirit**. 14 And we have seen and do testify that **the Father sent the Son to be the Saviour of the world**. 15 Whosoever shall confess that Jesus is the Son of God, **God dwelleth in him**, and he in God. 16 And we have known and believed the love that God hath to us. God is love; and he that dwelleth in love dwelleth in God, and **God in him**.*

Salvation in Daniel's Seventieth Week is Jesus, Jesus, Jesus! It is the blood that Christ shed for all mankind—His blood sacrifice is *not* limited to those in the Church Age but saves in the ages to come. The saint in the future will be saved by the blood, protected by the blood, and delivered by the blood. Have you trusted in that blood to save you?

Any teaching that detracts from Christ's sacrifice on the cross is of satanic origin and contributes to the future deception. Those today proclaiming a false gospel for the future are potentially condemning souls to Hell through the falsehoods they propagate. If you are here during this horrendous period, do not let the false teachings deceive you. Man's

ONLY means of salvation remains trusting in Jesus' sacrificial atonement.

Examining the Practical

The theological aspects already discussed concerning faith-plus-works salvation are most important. However, examining this subject from a ***practical*** perspective offers even more insights.

God "changes not" *(Malachi 3:6)* and is not inconsistent. Yet, some claim that He will allow "works" to play a part in an individual's eternal justification. Hypothetically speaking, what if this doctrine of "faith-plus-works" salvation was true? What would that look like in a practical sense?

If God saved believers in the Old Testament by faith-plus-works, then dedicated cultist are burning in Hell today only *because they were born in the wrong dispensation*! The only more *horrible decree* would be John Calvin's (Augustine's) doctrine of Limited Atonement and Unconditional election. The doctrines of the hyper-dispensationalist and Calvinist are not far from the other!

If faith-plus-works salvation was right during Old Testament times, then God ceases to be just. Would not the souls who "worked" for their salvation and died in the Church Age been saved had they lived under the Law? Could not God have made those souls live under the Old Testament covenant if He wanted all men to be saved *(1 Timothy 2:4)*? If God was changing His methods for eternal salvation, why didn't He put each man in the correct dispensation?

The tyrant god of Calvinism operates the same way as the hyper-dispensationalist's god. While He is electing some for salvation, He is choosing others without hope to be damned. The faith-plus-works teacher should consider how close his teachings are to Calvinistic theology. The result of the faith-plus-works doctrine produces a god who is both arbitrary and capricious concerning the salvation of souls. This god is not THE God of the Bible.

Both false doctrines are equally damnable when tried under the scriptural microscope. The legitimate Bible-believer must decide to believe the scripture as it stands over what his peers and mentors teach and believe. It is better to be right with God no matter how hard it is to dodge the *"fiery darts of the wicked" (Ephesians 6:16)*.

Tribulation Salvation for the New Testament Believer

Sometimes well-meaning men complicate spiritual matters, especially concerning the issues revolving around salvation. For instance, God designed salvation to have an absolute simplicity *(2 Corinthians 1:12)*! Yet, men often fail to take God as His word. Every believer knows that the work of the cross was complete; it was sufficient; it was final concerning the soul's salvation. Yet, cults, denominations and schisms are always proclaiming that their system serves as an improvement to what Christ accomplished. How blasphemous!

Every true Bible-believer agrees that no man gets to Heaven through their works. Why then would these same teachers claim that faith-plus-works save anyone during Daniel's Seventieth Week? Consider how ridiculous the matter. As absurd as it is to assert Old Testaments saints could keep the Law to be *eternally saved*, how much more foolish to proclaim salvation for anyone *post-Calvary* by *adding their works* to Christ's work on the cross. The eternal salvation of the soul is either all of God or man plays his part in attaining it.

> **Romans 11:6** *And if by grace, then is it no more of works:* **otherwise grace is no more grace***. But if it be of works, then is it no more grace:* **otherwise work is no more work***.*

How exactly are "Tribulation" saints saved by "faith-plus-works?" The hyper-dispensationalist should answer the same questions posed to any false teacher who teaches man's works can contribute to his salvation.

- What exactly are the "works" to be done for salvation?
- How many "works" are necessary for salvation?
- What if the "works" are below par; do they disqualify as insufficient?
- What about "works" done with impure motives; are these acceptable?
- Must the individual ultimately die in a state of grace to be saved?

God gave His Son Jesus Christ for the sins *of the whole world* for a reason—no man could earn salvation nor add to God's ultimate sacrifice. Those who teach otherwise, *especially after Calvary,* should consider the fallacy of such thinking. Does Christ's death on the cross become less efficacious after the Rapture?

Comparing scripture with scripture proves that faith-plus-works could never save Old Testament saints. Faith-plus-works has not been able to save one Church Age saint, no matter how much the cults proclaim it to be so. How careless for a professed Bible teacher to teach that those in the Age to come are saved in this manner! Such false teaching minimizes the cross of Christ!

The Lord Jesus Christ accomplished all this and more on the cross:

- HE became sin for us *(2 Corinthians 5:21)*
- HE paid for our sins *(Galatians 1:4)*
- HE died for us because we had nothing to offer God as payment for our sins *(1 Peter 3:18)*
- HE rose again for our justification *(Romans 4:25)*

What is *eternal salvation*? The answer is simple: it is the Lord Jesus Christ. It is not a prayer; not a formula; not even an altar call. Salvation is in the *person* of the Lord Jesus Christ. That fact is the reason God commands all men to receive His Son *(1 Timothy 2:4)*. In Him (and in Him alone) is salvation. Anyone who does not believe *solely* on the Lord Jesus Christ for salvation will not receive eternal life. He alone must be the object of man's belief and trust.

> **Ephesians 1:13 In whom** ye also **trusted**, *after that ye heard the word of truth, the gospel of your salvation:* **in whom** *also after that ye* **believed**, *ye were sealed with that holy Spirit of promise,*

This great truth for the Church remains valid even during the time of Jacob's trouble. It is impossible to trust in the Lord Jesus Christ and at the same time, believe that good works will save a soul and gain eternity. Any works added to the work of Christ diminishes His payment on the cross. Does the Bible offer any evidence of another kind of "Tribulation" salvation? No, none at all.

11
Conclusions on Salvation

FAR TOO MUCH of today's teaching and preaching reeks of spiritual shortsightedness. This lack of forethought is especially disconcerting when considering the eternal consequences to those who follow us. The preaching today (and that means the false teachings too) will influence souls during Daniel's Seventieth Week.

Pure motives are of utmost importance, but no guarantee that the outcome will be pure. It helps to examine why you believe certain things. What motivates you most? Are your actions directed by God or by your favorite teacher and your alma mater? The fundamental question is, "Who do you most seek to please?"

> **2 Timothy 2:4** *No man that warreth entangleth himself with the affairs of this life;* ***that he may please him who hath chosen him to be a soldier****.*

Man's propensity to never admit fallibility is one of Satan's greatest tools for hindering spiritual growth (pride). Every honest and sincere Bible student knows that only what the Bible truly teaches matters—not whether some teaching aligns with any other man's perspective. I have grown weary of being asked whether my teachings align with this man or with that one. Man worshipping carnality is on the rise **(1 Corinthians 3:1-4)**! I desire to strive always to teach correct doctrine and align with God and His holy writ. I want to allow the Bible to correct my errors and *never* fail in that endeavor for fear of man.

Souls Hang in the Balance

The saints in Daniel's Seventieth Week are promised supernatural salvation (as all salvation is supernaturally attained without any admixture of works). These believers are also promised supernatural protection and deliverance (but not necessarily a long life expectancy). Although some falsely teach that a faith-plus-works-setup can save a person in Daniel's Seventieth Week, the Bible nowhere condones such a fallacy.

Along with the 144,000 and the Two Witnesses, the Bible clearly states that an angel will be delivering the truth of the *"everlasting gospel"* **(Revelation 14:6)**. What happens if those teaching that a man's works are an essential element in salvation for the future turn out to be wrong? Those proclaiming faith-plus-works salvation will be condemning the ones who place their trust in a false gospel and false hope.

IF during Daniel's Seventieth Week people ARE saved by a faith-and-works-setup as some men proclaim, then condemnation would come to those who trust solely in Christ's shed blood **(Revelation 12:11)**. The primary purpose of this writing shows the hypothesis of faith-plus-works salvation to be patently false. It is dangerous and damning to the soul because it is unbiblical and souls hang in the balance. It is better to be right with God than to be accepted by man.

Salvation Always Involves Trusting in God

Salvation has always been and always will be *trusting* in God's revealed truth. Salvation is by *grace* because no one **deserves** salvation. Salvation is by *grace* because no one can **earn** salvation. Salvation is by *grace* through *faith;* otherwise, an individual could boast for their part played in the soul's redemption **(Ephesians 2:8-9)**. The salvation of the soul always points to the *unmerited favor* of God. Praise God He opened my eyes to this truth, and I have repented of teaching any faith and works salvation mixture.

A person in Daniel's Seventieth Week trusts in the Lord as witnessed by him calling upon the name of the Lord **(Acts 2:21)**. As a believer, he has become a part of the elect **(Mark 13:27)**, the brethren **(Revelation 6:11)**, and the saints **(Revelation 13:7)**. Through God's grace and supernatural protection, the saint during Daniel's Seventieth Week cannot be deceived, and thus he will not be deceived into taking the Mark of the Beast **(Revelation 14:11)**.

Believers caught by the authorities are not to fear their captors because God will put the very words into their mouths they need to speak **(Mark 13:11)**. God receives all the glory, and He has everything figured out. I only wish that I could say I always taught the truth in this manner. I didn't, and I was wrong! God give me a loud enough voice to undo the effects of having taught this particular error. My prayer is that God will stop the mouths of anyone trying to draw attention away from His mercy and His saving grace even if their teachings do not apply to the present day *(Titus 1:11)*.

An Enduring Legacy

Every preacher should strive for a God-glorifying legacy by trying to positively influence those living on the earth after the Church is gone.[1] Any other mindset is surely self-centered and potentially soul condemning. One of the most rudimentary ways to do this is by ensuring that if your teachings turn out to be unbiblical, you are brave enough to fix the wrongdoing. If (and when) something you have taught falls short of perfection, simply admit the error and fix the failings. NEVER allow pride to interfere with doing the right thing.

Every preacher's legacy should be that he loved souls enough to fix any of his errant teachings. That is what I want! I taught the things that were taught to me. I had to repent of these teachings, and humbly ask God to give me the courage to stand true to scripture. I also pray for a more significant influence to undo the wrongs caused by parroting erroneous teachings. The *ad hominem* attacks attempting to discredit my character have done nothing more than to strengthen my resolve to stand firm upon God's word *(Matthew 5:44)*.

---

[1] This departure of the Church would include the individual leaving at death or the Rapture of all believers.

12
False Pauline Preeminence

Colossians 1:18** And he [Christ] is the head of the body, the church: who is the beginning, the firstborn from the dead; that **in all things he might have the preeminence.

CHRIST MERITS THE preeminence in all things and never some mere mortal, not even the blessed Apostle Paul! Yet, because of his influence upon the church, some hyper-dispensationalists have stated that Paul deserves the preeminence. Hyper-dispensationalists are notorious for this such recklessness.

Every Bible student knows that God led Paul to write more books of the Bible than any other man. Yet, mere academic facts are not as important as the lessons learned from the specifics given concerning the man's life. Paul is no exception. For this reason, one should consider how Paul serves as one of the most significant personal examples of the desperate need for *living grace* following *saving grace*.

In considering this truth, one must study what Paul wrote concerning the Law. By inspiration, Paul wrote the right thing! Yet, his life revealed some serious flaws in failing to live according to what he wrote.

God led Paul to repeatedly write concerning the Law's inability to make a man righteous. He wrote that if justifiable righteousness for salvation could come from keeping the Law, then Christ's sacrificial death was needless and pointless.

***Galatians 2:19 For I through the law am dead to the law,** that I might live unto God.*

***Galatians 2:21** I do not frustrate the grace of God: for **if righteousness come by the law, then Christ is dead in vain**.*

If man could add ANYTHING to Christ's sacrifice for salvation, then the Father would have been guilty of needlessly sacrificing His Son upon the cross of Calvary. The facts are simple: keeping the Law saved no one. In fact, keeping the Law never added anything to one's salvation—past, present or yet in the future. Paul testified that he was a mere sinner saved by God's mercy and grace.

Far from Flawless

Even after salvation, Paul remained a man with the same human frailties that have plagued all men born into the world *(James 5:17; Acts 14:15)*. Paul would be the last person to claim the type of almost flawless life that some of his most loyal devotees claim for him. There is no immaculate conception. Interestingly, Paul used one word to encapsulate his lawful works under the Law—*dung*.

> ***Philippians 3:8*** *Yea doubtless, and I count all things but loss for the excellency of the knowledge of Christ Jesus my Lord: for whom I have suffered the loss of all things, and do **count them but dung**, that I may win Christ,*

Earlier in the passage, he described himself as blameless concerning the righteousness *"which is in the law."*

> ***Philippians 3:6*** *Concerning zeal, persecuting the church;* ***touching the righteousness which is in the law, blameless****. 7 But what things were gain to me, those I counted loss for Christ.*

Yet, Paul's testimony revealed that had he CONTINUED to trust in his works and position under the Law, this would have been trusting *"in the flesh."*

> ***Philippians 3:4*** *Though I might also have confidence in the flesh. If any other man thinketh that he hath whereof he* ***might trust in the flesh, I more****:*

Most authors reluctantly write concerning the personal failings of friends—this is not true concerning the authors of holy writ. The Bible never exaggerates the vices of the wicked, nor does it inflate the virtues of the believers. In fact, the record of Paul's life after salvation serves as a testament to the divine authorship of the Bible. The Bible offers readers an accurate understanding of every man's true nature—both the positive and the negative. God's purpose in recording the errors and sins of Bible characters serves to magnify the exhibition of God's grace in the life of every believer.

NOAH: After being spared from the flood, the Bible exposes his miserable sin of drunkenness.

ABRAHAM: God called Abraham "the *Friend of God*" *(James 2:23)*, but also expressed his lack of faith. He went down into Egypt for protection and raised a fleshly seed in the person of Ishmael.

JACOB was one of God's chosen ones, and yet the Bible tells of his scheming, crooked, and slippery ways.

DAVID: Every believer has become acutely aware of David, a man after God's own heart, who committed the soul-condemning sins of adultery and murder.

SOLOMON: The Bible says that when Solomon was old that his wives turned his heart away from God. Solomon died while serving false gods *(1 Kings 11:4-8)*. Obviously, Solomon was saved by grace through faith.

PETER was blessed to testify concerning the most amazing of truths. The Lord Jesus Christ said that He would build His church upon the confession made by the Apostle Peter *(Matthew 16:18)*. Yet, the Bible offers an additional narrative concerning his cursing and denying that he even knew the Lord.

PAUL: One would rightfully expect that the Bible would be as equally forthright concerning the Apostle Paul. Paul, with the best of intentions, put his self-will above the will of God, causing his ministry to be cut short.

Paul ended up in a Roman prison, where according to tradition, he was eventually beheaded. From a human perspective, Paul's disobedience and imprisonment cut short his life and ministry. Interestingly, Paul's failings exhibited God's patience, His grace and His long-suffering.

Paul's Humble Beginnings

The Bible introduced Paul (Saul) in Acts chapter 7 at the stoning of Stephen. As a persecutor of the church of Jesus Christ, Paul expressed great delight in the stoning death of Stephen. Only a few chapters later in the book of Acts, Paul, while on his way to Damascus, was gloriously converted to Christ. Paul became not only a believer but a fervent disciple of the Lord Jesus Christ.

God then sent him to Damascus to the home of a man named Ananias. God commissioned Paul to be the apostle of the Gentiles. Importantly, it was not the other Jewish apostles who commissioned Paul.

Paul was baptized in Damascus and not in one of the Jewish enclaves of Jerusalem or Judah. Paul was blessed with a unique ministry. His record as a Christian started in Acts chapter 9, and continued throughout the remainder of the book of Acts. Take note of what God tells Ananias concerning Paul (Saul).

> **Acts 9:15** But the Lord said unto him, Go thy way: **for he is a chosen vessel unto me, to bear my name before the Gentiles, and kings, and the children of Israel**: 16 For I will shew him how great things he must suffer for my name's sake.

Saul's destructive ways and hatred for the Jewish believers caused Ananias to be quite reluctant. God informed Ananias that Paul's primary ministry was to serve as the apostle of the Gentiles. The Bible offers further insights into Paul's first trip to the city of Jerusalem.

God Told Paul to Depart Jerusalem with Haste

> **Acts 22:17** And it came to pass, that, when I was come again to **Jerusalem**, even while I prayed in the temple, I was in a trance; and saw him saying unto me, **Make haste, and get thee quickly out of Jerusalem: for they will not receive thy testimony concerning me**.

God told Paul that those in Jerusalem would refuse his testimony concerning Christ. At the outset of his ministry, God told him that the Jews would NOT listen to him. Thus, God commanded him to hastily flee Jerusalem. His ministry was to be abroad—NOT in the city of Jerusalem and NOT primarily to the Jews.

The Lord warned Paul that Jerusalem was the wrong place for him. Paul no longer belonged there. Yet, Paul presented the Lord with what seemed like a legitimate counterargument. Paul was sincere about his desire to reach the Jews, and he believed himself to be uniquely qualified to bring them to Christ. Albeit, he was sincerely wrong because God had called him to another ministry.

> **Acts 22:19 And I said, Lord**, they know that I imprisoned and beat in every synagogue them that believed on thee: 20 And when the blood of thy martyr Stephen was shed, I also was standing by, and

consenting unto his death, and kept the raiment of them that slew him.

Like most of us, Paul wanted to fix the mess that he had created. He believed he was the best one to reach the Jews with the gospel. They all knew his earlier reputation of persecuting the believers. Even with God's explicit instructions, Paul questioned and second-guessed God's plan. The Lord told Paul to depart:

Acts 22:21 *And he said unto me,* ***Depart: for I will send thee far hence unto the Gentiles.***

God's command was clear-cut. Paul's ministry was NOT to be in Jerusalem. Yet, during Paul's ministry, he made four visits to that city. Each visit got him into trouble, with no real progress with the Jews.

He got into deeper trouble every time he allowed his zeal and his love for the Jewish brethren to control him. No matter how intense the enthusiasm and determination, God never gives a license to disobey. It is never right to disobey God in the face of clear and definite commands. God repeatedly told Paul NOT to return to Jerusalem.

An Effective Ministry is Always God-centric

God told Paul that the Jews were not going to listen to him. They were not to be his primary ministry. He was wasting his time and beating the air. Yet, Paul ignored God and got into trouble each time he put his own will ahead of God's will. Galatians emphasizes this same truth that became the key to the later experiences of the Apostle Paul. Here is the narrative of him going to Jerusalem 14 years after his conversion.

Galatians 2:8 *(For he that wrought effectually in Peter to the apostleship of the circumcision, the same was mighty in me toward the Gentiles:).* 9 *And when James, Cephas, and John, who seemed to be pillars, perceived the grace that was given unto me,* ***they gave to me and Barnabas the right hands of fellowship; that we should go unto the heathen, and they unto the circumcision***.

Those apostles whom God sent to speak to Paul and Barnabas, confirmed God's message and direction. Paul's ministry was NOT to be in Jerusalem. His ministry was to be towards the heathen (Gentiles)—not the Jews in Jerusalem. Paul seemed to believe that his willingness to be accursed from God for the Jews was a good excuse for disobedience to God. This lesson is for every Christian:

- Sincerity is never a substitute for obedience.
- Earnestness is never a substitute for obeying God's commands.

The Bible records three different occasions where Paul disobeys God's commands concerning Jerusalem, and God has to deliver him out of each mess. Paul received a definite command: do not go to Jerusalem but go rather unto the Gentiles.

Legalistic Vows Void of Obedience

Acts chapter 18 records one of Paul's missionary journeys as he arrived in the city of Athens. Here Paul took a Jewish vow in preparation for his Jerusalem trip.

Acts 18:18 And Paul after this tarried there yet a good while, and then took his leave of the brethren, and sailed thence into Syria, and with him Priscilla and Aquila; having **shorn his head in Cenchrea: for he had a vow.**

This same man taking this vow rightfully wrote that Christians are no longer *"under the law."* Yet, he was now shaving his head and taking a vow in a legal ceremony. All this so that he could enter the temple in Jerusalem. He knew better than being involved in these legalistic vows. He had no business compromising the truth. Paul was the one who wrote:

Galatians 2:19 For I through the law **am dead to the law**, *that I might live unto God.*

Galatians 2:21 I do not frustrate the grace of God: for **if righteousness come by the law**, *then Christ is dead in vain.*

Galatians 2:16 Knowing that **a man is not justified by the works of the law**, *but by the faith of Jesus Christ, even we have believed in Jesus Christ, that we might be justified by the faith of Christ, and* **not by the works of the law**: *for by the works of the law shall no flesh be justified.*

Yet, Paul's determination to reach his brethren according to the flesh caused him to take a legalistic Old Testament vow. He did this despite knowing that Christ nailed these ordinances to the cross, making them no longer useful. Yet, he put himself under a useless legal obligation.

Preeminence Belonging Only to Christ

This unfortunate act was just the beginning of a series of ill-advised practices by Paul. On the surface, these undertakings are quite sad to witness. Fortunately, when more fully considered, they each also allow God to exhibit His grace more fully. Regrettably, those giving Paul the unwarranted preeminence reserved for the Lord **(Colossians 1:18)** will look for every means to justify his every action. This misplaced exaltation is no better than the God-like status given to Peter or Mary by some.

Yet, some of the most unscrupulous preachers would wrest the scripture to teach that Paul's vow was him becoming all things to all men.

> **1 Corinthians 9:20 And unto the Jews I became as a Jew**, *that I might gain the Jews;* **to them that are under the law, as under the law,** *that I might gain them that are under the law;*

This type of reasoning sounds plausible on the surface; however, zealousness is NEVER an excuse for disobedience **(1 Samuel 15:22)**. A man's methods are never justified when not according to the direct will of Almighty God. Acts chapter 20 records Paul again going into Macedonia, where he had so much success among the Gentiles in the past.

> **Acts 20:1** *And after the uproar was ceased, Paul called unto him the disciples, and embraced them, and departed for to go into* **Macedonia**. *2 And when he had gone over those parts, and had given them much exhortation, he came into Greece, 3 And there abode three months.* **And when the Jews laid wait for him**, *as he was about to sail into Syria, he purposed to return through* **Macedonia**.

The chapter later reveals Paul's motive for speed. He hasted to Jerusalem for the Jewish feast day—Pentecost.

> **Acts 20:16** *Paul had* **determined** *to sail by Ephesus, because* **he would not spend the time in Asia**: *for* **he hasted**, *if it were possible for him, to be at* **Jerusalem the day of Pentecost**.

At the beginning of Paul's ministry, God told him to *"make haste"* **(Acts 22:17)** to get OUT of Jerusalem and yet Paul *"hasted"* to RETURN to Jerusalem. His purpose was to observe a Jewish feast day. Paul determined to sail past Ephesus because he would not spend time in Asia for he *"hasted"* to make it to Jerusalem on the day of Pentecost to fulfil his vow.

Nailed to the Cross

This same apostle knew that Christ nailed the Jewish ordinances to the cross. Paul rightfully preached about grace and grace alone—not including any human works. Salvation AND SERVICE were all about believing on Christ that justifieth the ungodly.

> **Colossians 2:14** *Blotting out the handwriting of* **ordinances** *that was against us, which was contrary to us, and took it out of the way,* **nailing it to his cross;**

Yet, Paul was willing to pass on his calling and pass up preaching opportunities to make it to Jerusalem in time for Pentecost—a legal Jewish holiday. Paul had no business ignoring his calling to reach the Jews. What benefit would Paul receive from observing one of the seven Jewish legal holidays of Pentecost? Absolutely nothing!

Paul Skipped Preaching Opportunities

Paul was DETERMINED to skip his calling to preach so that he could make it to Jerusalem to fulfil his vow. Paul determined to *"sail by Ephesus"* but had to stop, so he called together the elders of the Ephesus church and gave them the news.

> **Acts 20:22** *And now, behold,* **I go bound in the spirit unto Jerusalem**, *not knowing the things that shall befall me there:* 23 *Save that* **the Holy Ghost witnesseth in every city, saying that bonds and afflictions abide me**.

God's ministers repeatedly warned Paul along his journey not to go to Jerusalem. The Holy Ghost witnessed to Paul: STAY OUT OF JERUSALEM. That ministry in that location was assigned to others and not to Paul. Yet, Paul determined that he was going anyway and all along the way the Holy Ghost warned him. God was holding him back, inhibiting his movements, but he pressed on contrary to the will of God.

> **Acts 20:24** *But* **none of these things move me**, *neither count I my life dear unto myself, so that I might finish my course with joy, and the ministry, which I have received of the Lord Jesus, to testify the gospel of the grace of God.* 25 *And now, behold, I know that ye all, among whom I have gone preaching the kingdom of God,* **shall see my face no more.**

Paul testified that this was his last meeting; something lay ahead that would be the end of his public missionary endeavors. He then kneeled to pray. In essence, Paul was saying I am so zealous that none of you can move me away from disobeying God. The Holy Ghost told him not to go, but Paul said that doesn't affect me. Paul was DETERMINED because he had a "higher" plan than God.

Every Christian can appreciate Paul's sincerity; his determination to not be swayed by man. He had his mind made up and was going to pray about it. Paul had already settled the matter in his heart and soul, and prayer would not change his determination. Paul did not need to pray about anything that God has previously forbidden. He was not going to change God's mind by merely going through the spiritual motions without being spiritual. Prayer never fixes disobedience.

> ***Acts 20:37*** *And they all wept sore, and fell on Paul's neck, and kissed him, 38 Sorrowing most of all for the words which he spake, that they should **see his face no more**. And they accompanied him unto the ship.*

One can sense Paul's haste. In previous travels, Paul preached in city after city establishing churches. He preached in Galatia, Macedonia, Phillipi, Berea, Thessalonica, Corinth and Athens, spending weeks, and months and sometimes even three years in a single location. Paul's determination to hastily drive forward to Jerusalem meant that Paul never again established another church. In fact, the Bible does not record another of his sermons except for his testimony before the Sanhedrin and the judges. Paul's travels took a *"straight course"* reflecting a deemphasis upon preaching.

> ***Acts 21:1*** *And it came to pass, that after we were gotten from them, and had launched, we came with **a straight course unto Coos**, and the day following unto **Rhodes**, and from thence unto **Patara**: 2 And finding a ship sailing over unto Phenicia, we went aboard, and set forth. 3 Now when we had discovered Cyprus, we left it on the left hand, and sailed into Syria, and landed at Tyre: for there the ship was to unlade her burden* [the emphasis is a stop for non-spiritual reasons—to unload the ship's burden]. *4 And finding disciples, we tarried there seven days:* [not because he wanted to minister but because he couldn't get any transportation] ***who said to Paul through the Spirit, that he should not go up to Jerusalem.***

Again, God used the pitstop to tell Paul *"through the Spirit"* not to go up to Jerusalem. At this stop, Paul ended up around some disciples who were led THROUGH THE SPIRIT to command Paul not to go up to Jerusalem.

> ***Acts 21:11** And when he was come unto us, he took Paul's girdle, and bound his own hands and feet, and said, **Thus saith the Holy Ghost, So shall the Jews at Jerusalem find the man that owneth this girdle, and shall deliver him into the hands of the Gentiles*** [God sends another witness to warn of his fate]. *12 And when we heard these things, both we, and they of that place, besought him not to go up to Jerusalem* [others try to convince him not to go]. *13 Then Paul answered, What mean ye to weep and to break mine heart? **for I am ready not to be bound only, but also to die at Jerusalem for the name of the Lord Jesus.***

Every Christian should bravely and resolutely be willing to die for the Lord, but only if that is God's purpose and plan. Nobody should be willing to serve or to die in a place where God said NOT to go. Finally, Paul had his way. God sent messengers to warn him all along the way. Paul determined to go anyway. The Bible points out Paul's lack of success. Consider the import of the following passage: Paul starts by expressing his fruitful ministry among the Gentiles, and then the conversation turns to the problem with the zealousness of the Jews.

> ***Acts 21:18** And the day following Paul went in with us unto **James**; and all the elders were present. 19 And when he had saluted them, he declared particularly what things God had wrought **among the Gentiles by his ministry**. 20 And when they heard it, they glorified the Lord, and said unto him, Thou seest, brother, how many **thousands of Jews** there are **which believe**; and they are all **zealous of the law**: 21 And they are **informed of thee, that thou teachest all the Jews which are among the Gentiles to forsake Moses, saying that they ought not to circumcise their children, neither to walk after the customs.** 22 What is it therefore? the multitude must needs come together: for they will hear that thou art come.*

Toning Down and Compromising God's Message

James and the elders in Jerusalem advised Paul that he must tone down his message concerning the Law and the Jewish customs. Paul must compromise to be accepted by the Jews. The Jewish brethren inform Paul that the message that he preached among the Gentiles would be unacceptable in Jerusalem with so many zealous Jews. So, they mapped out a plan for Paul.

The Jews had heard that Paul instructed the saved Jews living among the Gentiles not to circumcise their children or to abide by the Law. Paul was to assure the Jews that all this was merely a false report. If Paul failed to compromise, he might cause a riot or a church split or some other calamity. Paul must compromise for the good of his Jewish brethren and not for the glory of God.

> **Acts 21:23 Do therefore this that we say to thee**: *We have four men which have a vow on them;* 24 *Them take, and* **purify thyself with them** [to abide by the requirements of the Law], *and be at charges with them* [by paying your share of a bloody sacrifice to be offered in the temple], *that they may shave their heads: and everybody may know that those things, whereof they were informed concerning thee, are nothing* [but what they were told was true]; *but that thou thyself also walkest orderly, and keepest the law* [Paul was the one who wrote repeatedly that believers are not under the Law]. 25 *As touching the Gentiles which believe, we have written and concluded that they observe no such thing, save only that they keep themselves from things offered to idols, and from blood, and from strangled, and from fornication.* 26 **Then Paul took the men, and the next day purifying himself with them entered into the temple**, *to signify the accomplishment of the days of purification, until that an offering should be offered for every one of them.*

The Apostle Paul entered in the forsaken temple—the one where God's glory had departed, and the veil had been rent from top to bottom. There was nothing in that temple for a New Testament believer, especially for one who knew what Paul knew. Paul went with these men, paid his charges, and entered into the temple. This narrative shows that Paul was a man subject to like passions like other men *(Acts 14:15)*. He too could be guilty of hypocrisy and willful disobedience.

Paul preached the grace of God at Antioch and witnessed the salvation of many Gentiles. News of this phenomenon came to Jerusalem. So, the leaders in Jerusalem sent a committee to investigate what was taking place. During this encounter, Paul took time to confront Peter concerning his hypocrisy.

Galatians 2:11 *But when Peter was come to Antioch, I withstood him to the face, because he was to be blamed.* 12 *For before that certain came from James,* **he did eat with the Gentiles**: *but when they were come, he withdrew and separated himself,* **fearing them which were of the circumcision.**

No Orthodox Jew would ever eat or fellowship with a Gentile except for those who understood the truth post-Calvary. Peter understood the liberty he enjoyed as a Jewish believer in Christ. Yet, when Peter saw these legalistic Jews, he withdrew from eating with the Gentiles for fear of them. Paul preached about the transgression of building the things destroyed by the Law.

Galatians 2:18 *For if I build again the things which I destroyed,* **I make myself a transgressor.**

When Peter was building up that wall of separation condemned by God, Paul rebuked Peter for his double standard. Paul's testimony:

Galatians 2:19 *For I through the law am dead to the law,*

Galatians 2:21 *I do not frustrate the grace of God: for* **if righteousness come by the law**, *then Christ is dead in vain.*

Paul wanted to win the Jews by disobeying God. The book of Acts shows the Apostle Paul doing the very thing that he condemned Peter for doing. There is no questioning his purpose or zeal. Paul attempted to appease the Jews by bringing an offering.

Acts 21:27 *And when the seven days were almost ended, the Jews which were of Asia, when they saw him in the temple, stirred up all the people, and laid hands on him,* 28 *Crying out, Men of Israel, help:* **This is the man, that teacheth all men every where against the people, and the law, and this place**: *and further brought Greeks also into the temple, and hath polluted this holy place.*

Of course, God was right! God's witnesses were right. Paul was not going to have an effective witness in Jerusalem. The Jews were determined to end Paul's ministry by ending his life.

Acts 21:30 *And all the city was moved, and the people ran together: and they took Paul, and drew him out of the temple: and forthwith the doors were shut.* 31 *And as* **they went about to kill him**, *tidings came unto the chief captain of the band, that all Jerusalem was in* an uproar. 32 *Who immediately took soldiers and centurions, and ran down unto them: and when they saw the chief captain and the soldiers, they left* **beating of Paul.**

Paul had the opportunity to give his testimony. And then in the 10th verse two chapters later, the narrative explains how precarious the situation.

Acts 23:10 *And when there arose a great dissension, the chief captain, fearing lest* **Paul should have been pulled in pieces of them**, *commanded the soldiers to go down, and to take him* **by force** *from among them, and to bring him into the castle.*

Paul's Freedom Cut Short

This story ended with Paul's ministry being cut short from a human perspective, with him ending up in the castle and then in prison. His choices deprived him of his liberty and ended his missionary endeavors.

How does God respond to Paul's disobedience? It is all of grace! God does not set Paul aside by putting him on a shelf. He does not cast him away. Does God treat Paul as a disobedient child walking contrary to God, too stubborn and bullheaded to be blessed any longer? No!

God simply demonstrated His grace, mercy and longsuffering like His manner is with other sinners walking contrary to the will of God. Thankfully, God reveals to us the end of the story. God is going to use Paul as an example of what His grace can do even amid disobedience.

Imagine the scene: Paul is in the castle; likely his hands are bound and his hopes dashed. He is defeated, discouraged, disillusioned, unhappy and maybe even ready to quit on God. In that dungeon, he recalled thirty years earlier when God told him to make haste to get out of Jerusalem. God said to him that the Jews would not accept his testimony. Imagine what Paul was wondering. What follows from God are some of the most gracious words ever spoken by Him to a disobedient man.

Acts 23:11 *And the night following* **the Lord stood by him**, *and said* **Be of good cheer,** *Paul: for as thou hast testified of me in Jerusalem, so* **must thou bear witness also at Rome.**

God did NOT say, "I saved you by my grace and called you to preach and write scripture, but now I am through with you." Indeed, Paul suffered for his bullheaded stubbornness. He was in jail because of disobedience to a clear, definite command of God followed by numerous warnings from God not to go to Jerusalem. He was now paying dearly for his disobedience. The Lord showed Paul the extent of His grace; His readiness to forgive.

His life ended as a prisoner, yet God used Paul's disobedience as the means for the most significant ministry of his whole career, so that Paul could say in **Colossians 1:6** that the gospel had been preached to the whole world through the ministry of those Paul led to Christ.

God's Grace Exceeds Man's Blunders

Paul wrote 14 of the 27 books of the New Testament with eight of these epistles penned after his Roman imprisonment. What is the outcome of Paul's imprisonment: the seven epistles which tell us practically everything we need to know about the church—the body of Christ. God took Paul's errors and mistakes and turned them into a glorious exhibition of His grace.

Paul's life and ministry exhibited the fact that the Bible exalts the grace of God and never exalts the man, even someone of Paul's stature. The more the Devil attempts to destroy the believer—the greater the opportunity for God to demonstrate His *living* grace. The Devil wants to debase the human heart as deep, and as low, and as black, as he can, but God uses these attempts to exalt the grace of God. God does not give us the record of a man's faults to debase the man but rather to exhibit God's wonderful grace. Paul would be the last one to claim any merit or admiration but proclaimed, *"by the grace of God I am what I am"* **(1 Corinthians 15:10)**.

Paul's actions and direct disobedience reflected that he considered his purpose and plan more important than God's will. He went to Jerusalem after being repeatedly told NOT to go. Paul did not want to wait on the omniscient God with His perfect plan. Paul wanted the opportunity to reach his peers—his brethren according to the flesh—the Jews. No doubt a most laudable endeavor, but what "if" God had everything under control with another plan and purpose? A far better plan and a far BETTER purpose?

The Hebrew Magna Carta

Paul had persecuted the Jewish believers, even compelling them to blaspheme *(Acts 26:11)*. Yet, unbeknownst to Paul, the all-knowing God already had a plan set in place. Paul's impatience forced him outside the perfect will of God. Paul thought that souls were more important than obedience. God knew all along that he would give Paul the opportunity he so desperately craved—a second chance with the Jews in a way that Paul could never have imagined!

While in prison, God led Paul to write his fourteenth epistle—the book of Hebrews. This book has impacted the whole church and especially the Jews for two millennia. God did not limit Paul's outreach to a relative few Jews in Jerusalem during Paul's day. Paul focused solely on reaching the Jews in Jerusalem, yet God's focus was much more comprehensive.

God led Paul to write the Magna Carta for the lost and saved Jews. Paul did not know God's plan, but God knew it all along. If God would have shown Paul his will in advance, would he have obeyed? Would he have been content to follow God's leading in the mission field? Would his missionary endeavors have covered more territory with more souls won to Christ? These facts are likely the outcome, yet that is not how God works.

Despite Paul's disobedience, God still used Paul to pen a book addressed to the Hebrews that has stood the test of time and saved and served many souls. Imagine what God can do with those who never presume to know more than Him. If God can still use Paul with his frailties and failures, can't God still use YOU too?

Jesus Christ is the one deserving of the preeminence. Those giving it to Paul are guilty of exalting a man to the place reserved for the Saviour. A good indicator of a false balance would be to count the number of times a preacher mentions Paul versus the numer of times He mentions Jesus. God forbid that any preacher should fail in giving Christ the preeminence IN ALL THINGS.

Postscript

THERE HAVE BEEN those who claim that the author changed his position on faith-plus-works salvation in other Ages for political reasons or for some other equally deceptive motive *(Psalm 38:12)*. God as my witness, these imaginations of men *(1 Chronicles 28:9; Proverbs 6:16-19)* are as far from the truth as the east is from the west. Those making false accusations know this to be the case but would never admit such.

Early in my ministry, I simply repeated the teachings taught to me, believing them to be right. I did not even know there was another side to the issue concerning the means and mode of salvation outside the Church Age until after I had written my first book published in 2000. When my position was challenged, I firmly stood my ground and considered the "opposition" ignorant of the deeper truths of scripture. I knew I was a Bible believer and considered that maybe they failed in this regard. I did not understand everything but believed my position defensible and certainly worthy of defending no matter the personal cost.

After extensively studying both sides of the issue, I came to realize that the faith-plus-works position was becoming increasingly indefensible. That which I thought neatly stood upon its own interpretative pillars was sinking in the sand upon which those "pillars" rested. There were too many times upon deeper investigation that the teachings were found to be faulty. This teaching turned out to be man's private interpretations of scripture. I sought to do the very thing I am asking of my reader. Allow the Bible to fix your doctrine! Tune out the noise! Listen to that still small voice *(1 Kings 19:12)*.

Please do not allow pride, political pressures, personal associations, or even alma-maters to stop you from admitting your errors and fixing what you can while you can. At the Judgment Seat of Christ, the God who knows all motives will have the final say and reward your work accordingly. Man's fiery darts may pierce the outward flesh but cannot touch the inner you unless you allow them to do so *(Galatians 5:25-26)*. Here is wise advice for all who have been first to speak concerning my alleged motives.

> ***Proverbs 18:17** He that is first in his own cause seemeth just; but his neighbour cometh and searcheth him.*

I could waste a bunch of time, energy and ink showing this man or that man a liar or deceiver or manipulator of the record, but I have a greater desire than self-defense. My desire is to hear *"Well done, thou good and faithful servant"* even if the hordes of Hell rise up against me. As a way to seek balance, I always try to remember that I serve at the pleasure of my Saviour and live to please Him.

> ***Revelation 4:11** Thou art worthy, O Lord, to receive glory and honour and power: for thou hast created all things, and **for thy pleasure they are and were created**.*

I stand accountable to God and Him alone whether in the past, in the present or in the future. I do not answer to those who would attempt to intimidate me to compromise the truth that I believe to be true. Yet, it is incredible how many enemies a person can accumulate by deciding that the truth trumps friendships and outweighs every association. Paul asked a simple question of the believers at Galatia who once loved him dearly but decided that he was now their enemy.

> ***Galatians 4:16** Am I therefore become your enemy, because I tell you the truth?*

Ditto! You can count me as *your enemy* or treat me as your friend, but I will not allow any man to cause me to compromise what I believe to be true. I love serving my Saviour but deplore the weaponization of social media and the associated lies. Those who enjoy doing this seem to want to make a name for themselves *(Genesis 11:4)*. God will reveal our motives one day. God help me to stand true!

Scripture Index

Genesis
Genesis 11:4 104

Exodus
Exodus 5:2 35
Exodus 14:13 24
Exodus 14:30 24
Exodus 15:2 24
Exodus 16:4 27
Exodus 16:35 69
Exodus 21:30 27
Exodus 34:6 41

Leviticus
Leviticus 26:3-4 25

Deuteronomy
Deuteronomy 13:13 34
Deuteronomy 25:1 30
Deuteronomy 30:9-18 26
Deuteronomy 30:11-14 27

Judges
Judges 2:10-12 35

First Samuel
1 Samuel 2:12 34
1 Samuel 3:7 34
1 Samuel 10:19 62
1 Samuel 30:24 iv

First Kings
1 Kings 8:32 31
1 Kings 19:12 103

First Chronicles
1 Chronicles 28:9 .... 36, 103

Second Chronicles
2 Chronicles 6:22-23 17
2 Chronicles 6:23 18
2 Chronicles 30:9 41

Ezra
Ezra 9:8-9 41

Nehemiah
Nehemiah 1:7-9 52
Nehemiah 9:17 41

Job
Job 1:6 65
Job 2:1 65
Job 2:3 79

Psalms
Psalm 9:10 36
Psalm 13:5 25
Psalm 27:1 25
Psalm 38:12 103
Psalm 51:12 25
Psalm 86:15 41
Psalm 91:1 70
Psalm 103:8 41
Psalm 111:4 41
Psalm 112:4 41
Psalm 116:4-6 41
Psalm 119:99 16
Psalm 130:3-4 16
Psalm 145:8 41

Proverbs
Proverbs 6:16-19 103
Proverbs 18:17 104
Proverbs 21:31 60
Proverbs 25:2 67
Proverbs 28:4, 7 28
Proverbs 29:18 28
Proverbs 29:25 44

Isaiah
Isaiah 49:25-26 59
Isaiah 53:6 70
Isaiah 59:2 37
Isaiah 64:6 70

Jeremiah
Jeremiah 9:3 35
Jeremiah 10:25 35

Jeremiah 15:21 64
Jeremiah 30:7 74
Ezekiel
Ezekiel 3:23 31
Ezekiel 39:9 14
Daniel
Daniel 3:16-17..................... 64
Daniel 8:24........................ 62
Daniel 11:31 62
Daniel 11:32 62
Daniel 12:9........................ 16
Joel
Joel 2:13 41
Joel 2:32 80
Jonah
Jonah 4:2 41
Malachi
Malachi 3:6 .... 63, 82
Matthew
Matthew 5:17...................... 28
Matthew 5:44...................... 87
Matthew 14:15-16................. 14
Matthew 14:19-21................. 69
Matthew 16:18..................... 90
Matthew 19:25-26................. 71
Matthew 24:4...................... 70
Matthew 24:5...................... 70
Matthew 24:11................. 66, 70
Matthew 24:13......... 57, 60, 61, 79
Matthew 24:15..................... 62
Matthew 24:15-18................. 65
Matthew 24:20..................... 62
Matthew 24:22............ 60, 69, 72
Matthew 24:23................. 67, 74
Matthew 24:23-24............. 62, 73
Matthew 24:24............ 68, 74, 79
Matthew 24:31............ 57, 60, 73
Matthew 26:39..................... 73
Matthew 26:52-54................. 59
Matthew 28:10..................... 66
Mark
Mark 10:17-23..................... 28
Mark 13:10-11................. 73, 75
Mark 13:11.................... 64, 86
Mark 13:13........................ 60
Mark 13:22.................... 73, 74
Mark 13:27........................ 86
Luke
Luke 1:6 30
Luke 10:25-28 29
Luke 16:19-23 37
Luke 18:31-34 22
Luke 21:12-15 .... 73, 75
John
John 1:10-13 33
John 4:23-24 iv
John 10:27-28 71
John 14:15 52
John 14:21-24 52
John 16:13 48
John 20:17 66
Acts
Acts 2:17-20....................... 80
Acts 2:21 .... 47, 80, 86
Acts 9:15-16....................... 91
Acts 9:42 61
Acts 13:39 18
Acts 14:15 98
Acts 15:10 50
Acts 18:5 44
Acts 18:18 93
Acts 20:13 94
Acts 20:16 74
Acts 20:16-17..................... 94
Acts 20:21 44
Acts 20:22-25..................... 95
Acts 20:24 44
Acts 20:37-38..................... 96
Acts 21:1-22................... 96–97
Acts 21:23-26..................... 98
Acts 21:27-32................. 99–100
Acts 22:17-20..................... 91
Acts 22:18 44
Acts 22:21 92
Acts 23:10-11.................... 100
Acts 23:11 44
Acts 26:11 102
Acts 27:39 74
Romans
Romans 2:7 32
Romans 2:13 17
Romans 3:19 17

Scripture Index

Romans 3:28 31
Romans 4:5 18
Romans 4:25 84
Romans 5:3 14
Romans 5:11 18
Romans 6:23 vi
Romans 8:16 52
Romans 8:35 14
Romans 9:6 46
Romans 9:8) 58
Romans 11:6 . . . . 41, 83
Romans 12:1-3 42
Romans 12:12 14
Romans 14:10 65
Romans 15:25-26 57
Romans 16:17-18 56

First Corinthians

1 Corinthians 1:6-7 44
1 Corinthians 1:20-21 39
1 Corinthians 2:1-2 44
1 Corinthians 3:1-4 85
1 Corinthians 3:3-4 23
1 Corinthians 3:13 65
1 Corinthians 9:20 94
1 Corinthians 11:19 15
1 Corinthians 14:33 16
1 Corinthians 15:10 101

Second Corinthians

2 Corinthians 1:4 14
2 Corinthians 4:3-4 70
2 Corinthians 4:6 38
2 Corinthians 5:21 84
2 Corinthians 7:4 14
2 Corinthians 13:13 57

Galatians

Galatians 1:4 84
Galatians 2:8-9 92
Galatians 2:11-12 99
Galatians 2:16-21 93
Galatians 2:18-21 99
Galatians 2:19-21 88
Galatians 2:20 53
Galatians 2:21 17
Galatians 3:21 18
Galatians 3:26 58
Galatians 4:8-9 38
Galatians 4:16 104
Galatians 5:25-26 104

Ephesians

Ephesians 1:13 84
Ephesians 2:6 55
Ephesians 2:8-9 86
Ephesians 2:9 21
Ephesians 4:12 57
Ephesians 4:15 39
Ephesians 4:30 52
Ephesians 6:16 82

Philippians

Philippians 1:14 61
Philippians 1:23 55
Philippians 3:3-9 52
Philippians 3:4-6 30
Philippians 3:4-8 89
Philippians 3:9 70
Philippians 4:19 74

Colossians

Colossians 1:2 57
Colossians 1:18 88
Colossians 2:14 95
Colossians 4:7 61

First Thessalonians

1 Thessalonians 3:4 14
1 Thessalonians 5:19 52

Second Thessalonians

2 Thessalians 1:4 14
2 Thessalonians 1:7-10 66
2 Thessalonians 2:1-4 77
2 Thessalonians 2:3 78
2 Thessalonians 2:4 65
2 Thessalonians 2:8 77
2 Thessalonians 2:9-10 75
2 Thessalonians 2:10-12 78
2 Thessalonians 2:11 76

First Timothy

1 Timothy 1:9 18
1 Timothy 2:4 . . . . 39, 82, 84
1 Timothy 2:14 68
1 Timothy 3:16 71

Second Timothy

2 Timothy 1:7 63
2 Timothy 1:14 41
2 Timothy 2:4 85
2 Timothy 2:18 23
2 Timothy 4:3 17

Titus
Titus 2:12 16
Titus 2:13 13

Hebrews
Hebrews 4:16 42
Hebrews 6:11 47
Hebrews 7:22-27 43
Hebrews 10:22 47
Hebrews 11:4-8 36
Hebrews 11:6 . . . . 37, 70
Hebrews 12:5-8 49
Hebrews 13:5 42
Hebrews 13:5-6 . . . . 71, 72
Hebrews 13:6 42
Hebrews 13:8) 63

James
James 2:18 32
James 2:23 90
James 4:8 60

First Peter
1 Peter 1:18-19 . . . . 19, 51, 65
1 Peter 2:24 19
1 Peter 3:7 52
1 Peter 3:18 84

Second Peter
2 Peter 2:1 17
2 Peter 2:1-2 18
2 Peter 2:9 16
2 Peter 3:18 39

First John
1 John 2:1 65
1 John 2:3-4 49
1 John 3:10 57
1 John 3:22-24 51
1 John 4:4 . . . . 14, 63, 81
1 John 4:13-16 81
1 John 5:1-5 50
1 John 5:13 42

Jude
Jude 1:24-25 43

Revelation
Revelation 1:2 45
Revelation 1:7 74
Revelation 1:9 . . . . 14, 45
Revelation 4:11 104
Revelation 6:9 . . . . 44, 45, 58
Revelation 6:9-11 . . . . 55, 66
Revelation 6:10 66
Revelation 6:11 . . . . 58, 86
Revelation 6:12 80
Revelation 7:9 . . . . 55, 58, 76
Revelation 7:14 . . . . 14, 55, 76
Revelation 9:20 56
Revelation 11:7 45
Revelation 11:13 57
Revelation 12:7-9 65
Revelation 12:9 . . . . 55, 79
Revelation 12:10 . . . . 65, 66
Revelation 12:11 . . . . 44–46, 81, 86
Revelation 12:12 . . . . 55, 65
Revelation 12:16 69
Revelation 12:17 . . . . . . 45, 48, 53, 56, 57
Revelation 13:3-4 67
Revelation 13:7 . . . . 55, 86
Revelation 13:8 75
Revelation 13:10 . . . . 57, 59, 61
Revelation 13:11-18 69
Revelation 13:12-14 68
Revelation 13:15-18 67
Revelation 14:6 . . . . 79, 86
Revelation 14:11 . . . . 67, 86
Revelation 14:12 . . . . 51, 53
Revelation 14:12-13 61
Revelation 14:13 . . . . 14, 58, 62
Revelation 15:2 67
Revelation 15:5 45
Revelation 16:2 67
Revelation 16:6 54
Revelation 16:9 56
Revelation 16:11 56
Revelation 17:8 75
Revelation 19:10 45
Revelation 19:11 67
Revelation 19:11-14 66
Revelation 19:15 66
Revelation 19:20 . . . . 67, 68
Revelation 19:21 57
Revelation 20:4 . . . . 65, 67
Revelation 20:15 18
Revelation 22:14 54

Word Index

A

abomination of desolation 65
accuser at Judgment Seat of Christ 65
ad hominem attacks 87
adopted 14
alma-mater 103
altar 58
apple analogy 23
assurance of salvation 49-50

B

beheaded 65
Belial not know the Lord 34
blameless in the Law 29-30, 52, 89
blending of works and grace 41
blood 15-19, 30, 45, 46, 51, 54, 57, 86
boast 21
bodies burn for 7 years 14
born again 33
brethren 51, 55, 57, 58, 66
buy and sell 63-69
buy one's salvation 28
by (twice not three times) 44-46

C

calling upon the name of the Lord 86
Calvinist similiarities 23, 49, 56, 70
children of Belial 34
circumcised 14
clergy 11
confessing false teaching 21
confusion 16
conscience 28
content of faith 16
context 24, 25, 27, 34
cultists 18
cults 28

D

Daniel's Seventieth Week 14, 70, 72, 85
date-setting 13
deceived 68, 72, 86
deception 9, 45, 54, 62, 67-75
delivered 47
die
    in his sin 31
    in the Lord 58
    in state of grace 57
disobedience brings a curse 26
Dispensational Salvation 9
dispensationalism defined 15
draw nigh unto God 60

E

egotism 48
eisegesis 13
elect 51, 57, 57, 66, 72, 86
element of faith and works 31-32
Eli's sons not know the Lord 34
endure unto the end 60-61, 79
enemy because tell truth 104
eternal security verses 42
everlasting gospel 86
Ezekiel
    die in his sins statement 31
    chapter 38-39 war 13

F

faith 32, 36, 38, 61
faith of Jesus 51-53
faith-plus-works 18, 21, 30, 44, 46, 48, 54, 61, 103
fallibility 85
false teachings 18
fellowservants 57, 66
fellowship severed 37, 44

fiery darts 103
filthy rags 70
free will 70
fringe group 44
fruit 47

G

gap after the Rapture 13
gathered by the angels 60
godly living 16
gospel not given in Deuteronomy 27
grace 80, 86
great multitude 76
great tribulation
    describes magnitude 14
    destination of believers 58, 76
Great White Throne hypothetical 18
grieve 52

H

Hall of Faith 36
haste 94
Hebrews
    chapter 11 37
    eternal security 71
    Paul's Magna Carta 102
    teachings contrary 42-43
    through Jude hyperdivided 19
heresy
    Christ's blood insufficient 15
    inconsistent teachings 19
    extolling virtues of good works 54
heretics 18
hindered 52
holy living 32
Holy Ghost 64, 75
hyperdispensationalist defined 16-17

I

"*if it were possible*" 73-74
imminence 13
in the Lord 14, 61
Israel 46

J

Jacob's Trouble 9
justification like James chapter 2 30-31

K

keep the commandments of God 48-56
    for assurance of salvation 49
    to get prayers answered 51
    to show you love God 52
    testify of relationship with God 53
keeping the Law 89
knew not God 38
knowing the Lord relationship 33-36
knowledge not intellectual 34
knowledge of the truth 39
known of God 38

L

laity incorrect use 11
Law
    not give to justify anyone 18
    prolonged life 26
lawyer not saved by works 29
laymen incorrect use 11
Lazarus Old Testament 37
living grace 88
looking forward to the cross 22-7
Lordship Salvation 61
love 52

M

Magna Carta: Hebrews 102
manna 69
Mark of the Beast 9, 14, 64, 67
marksmanship 60
martyrs 64
meditate 75
mentor pleasing 23
Michael the archangel 55, 65
militia 61
Moses' books salvation 31
motives 103, 104
multitudes 76
mutation after cross 45
mutually exclusive works and grace 41

N

Nehemiah 52
newspaper 13
Nicolaitans 11
Noah saved by building a boat 24

not naming names 17
novice 23

O

obedience 26
Old Testament
    means of salvation undefined 21-22
    longer life under the Law 26
    the 613 laws 50
Olivet Discourse 62, 70
overcame 46
overcomers trust in Christ's blood 44

P

Paradise 37
parroting 87
Paul 88
paid for salvation 27
peer pleasing 23, 71
Pentateuch 32
physical 30
    deliverance 62
    lives 29
    longevity 26
    salvation 23, 25
please God only by faith 37
pleasure 104
political reasons 103
Post-Calvary salvation 22
prayers answered 51
precursors 13
preeminence 88, 94, 102
preppers 60
private interpretations 103
Progressive Revelation 16
purgatory falsely implied 28, 65

Q

quench 52
questions 10, 11

R

reading New Testament into Old 32
relationship knowing the Lord 34
remnant 56, 57
rich young ruler ignored 28-29
rightly dividing while fleeing 42
root 47

S

saints 55, 57
salvation contexually 23, 24, 25, 30
salvific defined 19
Samuel 34
Satan's last hurrah 65
seduce 74
self-defense 59, 104
self-reliance saves 80
setup (faith-plus-works) 21
Shadrach, Meshach, and Abendnego 64
shortening of the days 72
social media weaponization 104
societal turmoil 13
Solomon told to know the Lord 36
sons of Belial lost 34
soteriology 15
souls deemed less valuable 19
stewards 15
strong delusion 76
supernatural protection 85

T

temporal 30
temporal condemnation 18
testimony
    defined 44-45
    of Jesus Christ 56
throne of grace 43
trans-dispensational truths 38
Tribulation
    always suffered 14
    books falsely so called 42
    period inaccurate 14

V

vow 93

W

weaponization of social media 104
willful disobedience 98
woman 53, 55, 56
word of their testimony 44, 46
works fruit of salvation 21
works-plus-faith 32
wrest 46, 48

Notes